Prolific writer and missiological anth
economist and political scientist Rasl
story of Afghanistan, including its hi.
strong theology of culture, and hope in the resurrection, renewal, and restoration, the
authors provide riveting stories of Afghans finding hope amidst devastation and danger
as followers of Jesus. Practical suggestions for supporting refugees and immigrants
abound, and the kingdom vision of Revelation 7:9, of people from every language and
culture worshiping together around the throne of God, animates this essential book.

DARRELL WHITEMAN, PhD
CEO, Global Development

This book is an absolute treasure! The authors give us more than beautiful glimpses of
Afghans and Afghanistan, they awaken us to the beauty of the mystery of Christ and
the often-paradoxical ways that Jesus is transforming lives in some of the most difficult
and broken places of our world. I pray that many churches in the US and Europe would
read this book and catch a vision of how to reach the thousands of Afghan refugees that
God has brought into our neighborhoods with the Good News of Jesus.

REV. SASAN TAVASSOLI, PhD
Senior Lecturer, PARS Theological Center

In 1953 some twelfth-grade students in one of the most prestigious high schools in
Kabul told me they were incensed at the *Encyclopedia Britannica*, which had indicated
that Afghanistan was 99 percent Muslim. "No!" they insisted. "Afghanistan is 100%
Muslim!" They could not conceive of an Afghan who was not Muslim. Today there is a
growing, if tentative, body of believers in Jesus Christ, living carefully as good citizens
under the radar of most news organizations. This book is an exciting report on what is
going on now in the religious life of the country.

ROBERT CANFIELD, PhD
Professor Emeritus, Washington University

Gripping, informative, thoughtful, and beautifully written, Adeney and Aalish peel
back the layers of Afghanistan, holding each one up to the light of Jesus. Replete with
moving and memorable stories, *Afghan Mountain Faith* is a gift to the church and the
people of Afghanistan, offering a pathway forward as their destinies intersect.

DAVID GARRISON
Author, *A Wind in the House of Islam*

Afghanistan is a beautiful country with a rich culture and an incredibly difficult history.
The recent resurgence of the Taliban has exacerbated the suffering of the Afghan
people but has also resulted in the movement of many refugees from their homeland—
among the most dangerous places in the world to follow Jesus—into countries blessed
with religious freedom, where Afghans can consider the claims of Christianity for
themselves, without governmental restrictions or interference. For Christians seeking
to welcome, love and convey the hope of the gospel, Miriam Adeney and Rashid
Aalish's *Afghan Mountain Faith* is an indispensable resource.

MATTHEW SOERENS
World Relief Vice President, Advocacy and Policy

Of the top three Christian books I recommend on Afghanistan, this is now in first place. The authors embed their cultural analysis within a global theology on the subjects of culture, Islam, and Afghanistan. They address the role of women and women's rights, depraved aspects of Afghan culture, and the six types of Islam with sensitivity and clarity, naming the good and the evil. They explain and analyze Afghan culture in a redeeming way, without resorting to patronizing, syncretism, nationalism, or exceptionalism. In every chapter of this book, the authors tell a third story, one that reveals our shared experiences as humans and as Christ followers.

ANNA HAMPTON, DRS
Global Risk Consultant, Barnabas International
Author, *Facing Fear* and *Facing Danger*

Growing up in India, I was introduced to the Afghani people through Tagore's *Kabuliwallah*. In recent years, as my work has taken me across Europe, North America, and Asia, I have met several of them, and have heard stories of how these beautiful people are becoming followers of Jesus. May this inspire you to get involved with refugees, immigrants, and other diaspora peoples around you.

SAM GEORGE, PhD
Catalyst, Lausanne Movement
Co-editor, *Refugee Diaspora*

Afghan Mountain Faith had me hooked on the first page. From the many heart-pounding God-sized stories to practical wisdom and insight, this refreshing read has something for everyone—laypeople and church planters alike. This book inspired me to expand my compassion for Afghanis everywhere.

KAREN BEJJANI
Co-Founder, iHOPE Ministries

Afghan Mountain Faith captured my attention with the singular combination of historical fact, spiritual context, and unflinching truth. The authors describe an apparently failed nation, but also explain how the world powers moved into the vacuum in their nefarious abuse of geography and culture to organize and exploit Afghanistan for their own benefit. The entire book comes alive as it interweaves the narrative fabric of personal stories. And I love the way it lands, with practical recommendations for churches, ministries and families around the world who receive Afghan (and other) refugees.

WILLIAM TAYLOR, PhD
Executive Director Emeritus, World Evangelical Alliance Mission Commission
President, TaylorGlobalConsult

"Where sin increased, grace increased all the more" (Rom 5:20). Since the Islamic revolution in Iran, hundreds of thousands of Iranians have come to Jesus Christ as their Lord. Now is the time for Afghans. God is taking away the veil from their eyes to come into His marvelous Light. Many are disillusioned and are open to the Good News. *Afghan Mountain Faith* is a very timely and comprehensive tool for any Christian who wants to share Christ's love with Afghans whom God has brought near them.

MOHAMAD REZA ROSHANZAMIR
Co-Founder, Elam Ministries

AFGHAN MOUNTAIN FAITH

Stories of Justice, Beauty, and Relationships

Miriam Adeney & Rashid Aalish

I hope you enjoy reading this book!

WILLIAM
CAREY
PUBLISHING
visit us at missionbooks.org

William Carey Publishing (WCP) publishes resources to shape and advance the missiological conversation in the world. We publish a broad range of thought-provoking books and do not necessarily endorse all opinions set forth here or in works referenced within this book. WCP can't verify the accuracy of website URLs beyond the date of print publication.

All Scripture quotations, unless otherwise indicated, are taken from the Holy Bible, New International Version®, NIV®. Copyright ©1973, 1978, 1984, 2011 by Biblica, Inc.™ Used by permission of Zondervan. All rights reserved worldwide. www.zondervan.com. The "NIV" and "New International Version" are trademarks registered in the United States Patent and Trademark Office by Biblica, Inc.™

Scripture quotations marked NLT are taken from the Holy Bible, New Living Translation, copyright ©1996, 2004, 2015 by Tyndale House Foundation. Used by permission of Tyndale House Publishers, Carol Stream, Illinois 60188. All rights reserved.

Published by William Carey Publishing
10 W. Dry Creek Cir
Littleton, CO 80120 | www.missionbooks.org

William Carey Publishing is a ministry of Frontier Ventures
Pasadena, CA | www.frontierventures.org

Cover and Interior Designer: Mike Riester

ISBNs: 978-1-64508-542-3 (paperback)
        978-1-64508-544-7 (epub)

Printed Worldwide

27 26 25 24 23   1 2 3 4 5   IN

Library of Congress Control Number: 2023947628

Contents

— Chapter 1 —

The Toughest Country in the World

"Are you willing to renounce the claim that Jesus is God?"

Qazi Abdul Karim stood alone in a court of law. Over by the wall was a swordsman, blade at the ready. What would Qazi answer?

He was not raised poor or ignorant. His father was a judge, and his home was comfortable. When Qazi became an adult, he had traveled across the boundary that divides Afghanistan from Pakistan, a barrier that many Pashtun people feel is artificial. In Pakistan Qazi had found a job on the staff of a hospital.

There he discovered that many of his colleagues cared for the sick because they were motivated by the love of God expressed in Jesus. As Qazi heard more about Jesus—his life story, his teachings, his death and resurrection, his magnificent kingdom, and Jesus's personal love for him—Qazi's heart opened. Jesus became his Lord.

This was such a transforming experience that Qazi couldn't keep it to himself. Wherever he went, in markets, on buses, or in coffee shops, he talked about Jesus. He spread the story up and down the frontier that Pakistan shared with Afghanistan. Qazi became well known for his witness.

Back home, religious leaders were alarmed. "A disgrace!" they stormed.

Why? What was wrong with witness to Jesus? After all, Muslims consider Jesus a holy prophet.

Worshipping Christ as God is forbidden, and Muslims must not convert to other faiths. Conversion introduces chaos, the religious leaders believed. A totally Muslim community is the best environment for human flourishing. By contrast, a community with diverse faiths opens the door to ethical relativism and moral looseness. When Qazi talked about Jesus as Lord, that is what the religious leaders pictured.

"Something must be done to stop this before it goes further," they decided. So men were sent to arrest Qazi and transport him back across the border.

"Are you willing to renounce the claim that Jesus is God?" they challenged him. Qazi was not.

A seventy-pound chain was looped around his neck. A bridle was put in his mouth. Then Qazi was forced to march, pulling that chain three hundred miles from Kandahar to Kabul. People threw insults and mud and stones at him along the way.

In the Kabul courtroom he was again invited to return to Islam. When he refused, a ghastly scene unrolled: the swordsman lifted his weapon and slashed off Qazi's right arm.

As Qazi reeled from the shock and pain, and as blood dripped onto the floor, the judge challenged him again: "Recite the creed, 'There is no God but Allah and Muhammad is his prophet.' That is all you need to do."

But Qazi would not deny Jesus as Lord. Jesus was the center of his life. He would not swear loyalty anywhere else.

The swordsman sliced off his left arm. When Qazi still continued to affirm Jesus as Lord, he was beheaded.

Twenty-five years later, an Afghan man traveling in Iran met a Christian there. He wanted to talk about Qazi. "I was there in the court that day," the Afghan remembered. "I was a boy of ten or twelve at the time, but I have never been able to forget it. I saw a man tortured and hounded to death for his faith. He was a Christian. The remembrance of the light of peace on his face remains with me to this day. I can never forget it. Tell me the secret of it."

That Afghan became a follower of Jesus, and eventually returned to Afghanistan. Even a quarter century after his death, Qazi's life was still speaking.[1]

Through the centuries, many people have been punished harshly in this land, and not only Christians. Islamic law's most extreme version calls for cutting off the hands of thieves, stoning adulterers, and beheading other criminals. The powerful nations that wrested control here often had reputations for cruelty. Whether Mongols, Central Asian tribes, Russians, Chinese, Pakistanis, or, most recently, Americans flailing through twenty years of war, none have had outstanding reputations for gentleness and humaneness. The current ruling party, the Taliban, grew from orphaned boys and young men raised without the civilizing and softening influences of home and family. Even more extreme than the Taliban are the violent members of ISKP.

It is in this volatile context that Jesus's people have been killed for their faith. According to the *2022 World Watch List* published by Open Doors, Afghanistan is the hardest country in the world in which to be a Christian.

1 Wilson, *Afghanistan*, 122.

But times are changing. Millions of Afghan people are moving out of their homeland. Eighty thousand Afghan immigrants are expected in the US in 2023.

Many Americans would like to forget about Afghanistan, particularly the long years of war and the shabby end to that conflict. "Thank God that's over!" we may murmur with a sigh of relief. Yet as Afghan immigrants walk down our streets, shop in our malls, and send their children to our schools, it becomes apparent that Americans cannot wipe Afghanistan off the slate of our minds. The people are here—fellow human beings living together with us.

The people who remain in Afghanistan have not fallen off the map either. They wake up in the morning, wash their faces, slip on their sandals, open the door to go out and use their skills and resources to earn something and bring home food, and meanwhile stay as safe as they can. Children who are lucky enough to have a school nearby will wrestle with reading and math, polishing skills and general wisdom. Life spirals on. Afghanistan is not "over." The Afghan people are not finished, whether here or there.

What Is This Book About?

This is a book about relationships, justice, and beauty.

Relationships

There are many things seriously wrong with the world and with the church. There are many dangerous elements and flash points that could lead to disaster. And human beings are just as short-sighted and self-centered as ever, despite our educational and technological progress. On some days the future looks dystopian. At a more mundane level, gas prices are up. Egg prices are up. Housing costs are up. Whatever the long-term future may be, just now we are scrambling to stay in place.

Yet God has blessed us with friends, family, music, food, nature, sports, free schools, clinics and hospitals, pets, and our local churches, with their worship and teaching and fellowship and service opportunities.

Right in the middle of the complex reality where we find ourselves, God calls us into relationship with Him and with people. We have been born and set here at this point in space and time for God's purposes. We are not made for small things. We are meant for more. We have been empowered to bless the nations.[2]

---

2 God has called and empowered his people to bless the nations. Abraham received a commission: "All peoples on earth will be blessed through you" (Gen 12:3). During the exodus, God told Moses: "You are to love those who are foreigners, for you yourselves were foreigners in Egypt" (Deut 10:19). David sang, "May all the peoples praise You. May the nations be glad, for you rule the peoples with equity." Following Jesus's time on earth, Paul, John, and Peter were equally emphatic about God's care for all peoples and our responsibility to share the good news with them (See Acts 26:17; Rom 1:16; Eph 2:12, 13, 19; 3:6; 1 Pet 2:9–10; Rev 7:9–10).

At the heart of the universe there is a center. Ephesians 1:8–10 speaks of the ultimate mystery of the ages—that God will bring all things in the cosmos together in Christ. He is the cosmic fulcrum. God hears each of our groans, and from his eternal center he is drawing all of us, from all peoples and all dimensions of life, lifting us together, smoothing the sharp edges, weaving a pattern, tuning a harmonious symphony, nourishing a flourishing ecosystem in which every person finds a place. In Christ everything in the cosmos is being knit together.

This is the mystery at the core of reality. And although it is unfathomably large and incomprehensibly complex, it is also personal. In God's grand unity, we do not lose what makes each of us unique. Individual persons have a purpose, according to Ephesians 1:12, and that is to live for the praise of God's glory. We are not robots. We are not statistics. We have a sacred calling, a vocation, an anointing—to live with all of our gifts and quirks for the glory of God. Whether citizens or refugees, we are not marginal. Related to God and to each other, we experience empowerment to pour out our life's energies as we love our neighbors and work toward the kingdom of God.

But why Afghans? There are many other "neighbors" who need attention. Why focus on the people of Afghanistan? That question leads to the next section: justice.

Justice

This is a book about justice. At this moment in history Afghans are vulnerable, and God loves the vulnerable. Back home, most Afghans lack food. Some are starving to death. Yet, while the land is largely treeless, it is not barren. Wheat grows well. In fact, this may be the place where wheat was first domesticated. Gardens and fields are enriched by topsoil blown in annually on strong winds from Central Asia. Still, the temperature is cold and there are many mountains.

More devastating than the weather and topography is the collapse of international aid.

Russia invaded in 1979. Then came the Taliban, then the Americans, and now again the Taliban and another terrorist group known as ISKP. Given all this turmoil, the infrastructure and economy have been blown up repeatedly. Badly damaged, Afghanistan came to rely on foreign aid. Until mid-2021 it was receiving $8.5 billion a year. This made up 40 percent of its GDP.[3] When the Taliban seized power in August 2021, the aid ended abruptly. Since then, hardly any nations have recognized the Taliban as the legitimate government. As a result, foreign banks balk at doing business here, and international trade has dried up.

---

3 "The Next Crisis," *Economist*, 46.

Afghans are vulnerable not only economically but also socially. Women who previously ran their own businesses, taught, or studied now find themselves shuffled to the margins. The current regime has imposed a strict, fundamentalist version of Islam that limits women in public life. That means that half the population is largely shut down. This is particularly hard on widowed mothers whose income may make the difference between life and death for their children.

Most of all, Afghans are vulnerable because they have had so little chance to hear the good news.

Yet new things are happening. Because of the internet and because many Afghan people have fled their country and spread across the earth, it is easier than ever to share the gospel of Jesus with them. Human barriers never have controlled God, of course. God has spoken to people everywhere throughout time by means of nature, conscience, and dreams and visions. As Psalm 19:1–4 says, "The heavens declare the glory of God, the skies proclaim the work of his hands. Day after day they pour forth speech, night after night they reveal knowledge. They have no speech, they use no words; no sound is heard from them. Yet their voice goes out into all the earth, their words to the ends of the world."

In our time, however, Afghans have fresh opportunities to learn about Jesus, the center of the cosmos. This is their moment. We are privileged to be part of it. Focusing on Afghans at this point in history is fair. It is justice. Can we hide behind excuses like "I have other concerns"? Will we dribble out our lives for selfish goals, or will we stretch, genuinely bless the needy, and count for something?

Beauty

This is also a book about beauty. When God made the world, he set in motion a kaleidoscope of cultures, dazzling in their diversity. From the very beginning God said that it was not good for people to be alone (Gen 2:18). We were designed to live in communities of meaning. So God gave his blessing to human culture, and specifically to cultural areas like the family, the state, work, worship, arts, education, and even festivals. He gave attention to laws which preserved a balanced ecology, ordered social relations, provided for sanitation, and protected the rights of widows, orphans, foreigners, the poor, and debtors. He affirmed the physical world, out of which material culture takes shape. This does not mean God intended all cultures to be the same. No, he made us creative in his image so we could shape unique and varied lifeways, resulting in the mosaic that adorns his world.

Afghan culture is novel. Afghan people are not just producers, consumers, or victims who are interchangeable with everybody else in the world. They have their own heritage. In this context they live and laugh and cry and love.

So, in chapters 3–6 we pay them the respect of taking time to learn about their culture. It is true that there are a variety of Afghan cultures within the larger whole. It is also true that cultures change continually. Yet a core continuity flows on, a precious heritage that is as beautiful as the mountain ranges and carpets of this land.

From these Afghan people God deserves praise. The Lord of the universe is worthy of Afghans' awe. This is our deepest motive for mission—not just counting churches, nor feeding the hungry, but cultivating worship to the Lord of all creation from every part of his earth. Then cultural beauty will unfurl into cosmic beauty, mediated by a beautiful church. In spite of all the church's shabby shortcomings, it is going to be represented around the throne of God at the end of time by people from all ethnic groups and tribes and kindreds and nations, and God will take great pleasure in this diverse worship. That will include Afghans. What a magnificent scene it will be.

This book is about relationships, justice, beauty, and the Afghan people in God's kingdom.

Where Will You Journey in This Book?

Chapter 1 is an introduction. Chapter 2 sparkles with never-before-recorded stories of Afghans who are following Jesus. We discover their questions, the bridges that draw them, and the challenges that threaten them along their journeys.

Chapters 3–6 explore Afghan culture—patterns of material things, family, politics, and religion. Gospel themes are woven throughout. Theology of creation care, theology of culture, including affirmation and confrontation. Bridges for sharing the Lord Jesus Christ in the context of a Muslim worldview.

Chapter 7 shows how to bless refugees. Two families' stories—Rashid's and the Smythe's—frame the data, the resources, the steps, and the strategies, as well as the objections of people who feel this is a misplaced priority.

Chapters 8–10 return to Afghan believers, not simply as individuals but as members of communities who worship Jesus, and not simply as converts but as maturing disciples. Ministry resources are cited and approaches are described. Many issues arise, such as marriage, child raising, ethnic identity, and the temptations of a modern secular environment. Alongside chapter 8's effective strategies chapter 9 features worship. Four strong stories wrap up chapter 10.

Ultimately this book applies beyond Afghanistan. Christian missiologists everywhere wrestle with perplexing issues, and many of those are explored in these pages, relating to Islam, gender, ecology, disciple-making movements, church planting, orality, ethnodoxology, diasporas and migrants, multiethnicity, media, etc. Any missiologist can benefit from these reflections.

What will you take away from this book? Different readers will access different assets. If you want strategies to help refugees or to witness or disciple, there are strategies. If you want stories, there are stories. If you want systemic wrestling with stubborn missiological issues, that is here too, in a brief and accessible package. Audaciously we believe that if you are discouraged about the world or the church, you will not be after you read this book.

Is There Hope for Afghanistan?

Has Jesus ever been worshipped widely in Afghanistan? Yes. Over a thousand years ago there were many believers in this land. At the feast of Pentecost in Jerusalem shortly after Jesus left his earthly body and returned to heaven, Peter preached boldly, empowered by the Holy Spirit. Pilgrims from many nations were present at that feast and heard the good news that God has come close to us in Jesus. Thousands were moved and believed and were baptized (Acts 2). After they concluded their business in Jerusalem, they dispersed to their homelands. For some that meant traveling east along the Silk Road. Right next door to Afghanistan, in Iranian cities like Meshed, bishops and seminaries and local congregations were established. In Afghanistan itself in cities like Herat there were monasteries and cloisters and mission-training schools. Old Afghan coins bear an inscription "In the name of the Father, Son and Holy Ghost, one God." Ancient Afghan rug patterns display crosses.

What happened? Where did all this Christian community go? Tragically, the Bible was not translated into any Afghan language. That seems to make a difference in church history. When the Bible is accessible and studied by local people in their own language, the church will mature and endure. But when the Scripture is accessible only to clergy elites, even though the word may be honored, the church can die out. In this case, when Mongols from the east and Muslims from the west swarmed over the land, the light of the gospel flickered and burned low. The church became invisible as an institutional force. Still, Christians outside the country prayed and occasionally visited during the centuries that followed.

Kabul Christian Community Church was established in 1952. At that time Afghanistan was a monarchy. World War II had concluded not long before. In spite of the enormous tragedies of that conflict, the post-War period opened possibilities for change. Many nations declared their independence. In a great burst of energy and creativity and hope, and perhaps desperation as well, peoples worldwide began building roads and dams and schools as well as new governments. Afghanistan was a landlocked country in central Asia with one of the lowest literacy rates in the world. The needs of this nation pulled at the heartstrings of a few humanitarians.

In particular, Christians cared. They believed that people are more than animals or machines. Every person is formed to know God. They also believed that God in Jesus is the center of the cosmos. If few Afghans had even heard about this, then these people deserved particular attention. For physical, social, and spiritual reasons, a scattering of foreign Christian professionals, especially medics and educators, volunteered to make the long trek and settle down in Afghanistan.

In 1951, J. Christy Wilson and his wife Betty arrived. At that time the Minister of Education was looking for English teachers. Wilson was appointed to the oldest secondary school in the country, Habibia High School. For the next twenty-two years, Christy and Betty would live here. Among Wilson's various responsibilities he taught English to the prince, King Zahir Shah's son.

For their worship services, the foreign Christians were meeting in homes. Since Christians consider a community of believers to be a church, they viewed themselves that way, even though they had no building. Wilson had a PhD from Edinburgh, as well as graduate degrees from Columbia University and Princeton Theological Seminary. He officiated at weddings, funerals, and other ritual events in the international community. In 1952 the group invited him to become their pastor.

Around this time, an Islamic mosque was erected in Washington DC. This was intended to serve Muslim visitors to the US. Back in Afghanistan, Christians pondered: Why not a reciprocal arrangement here? Because foreigners were not allowed to own property, the Christian community requested a ninety-nine-year lease on a piece of land where they could build a church. This application was filed in 1957. It was denied. They waited two years and tried again. In 1966, after many complications, oral permission was granted by the prime minister's office, and subsequently approved by the Municipality of Kabul.

To reflect the shapes of mountains pointing skyward in Afghanistan, an A-frame building with side wings was designed by New Zealander and Afghan architects. The bishop of Lahore in Pakistan traveled to Afghanistan to join the team that solemnly stuck shovels into the dirt and turned over the first sod. By 1970 the church was mostly completed. When it was dedicated, hundreds attended. In the following years, this building became a center for prayer, praise, Scripture reading, teaching, discipleship, fellowship, and mutual encouragement. Two hundred people became regular worshippers.

Meanwhile, throughout the first half of the twentieth century there was a circle of praying people located just outside the borders of Afghanistan. Flora Davidson from Scotland was one of these prayer warriors. During her forty years of joyful service to Afghans, she and a Danish nurse traveled all along the borders to meet personally with others who were praying. In 1924 Flora had begun a monthly publication, *Afghan Prayer Circle*, which continued into the 1970s with a circulation of five hundred.

But fundamentalist Muslim factions stirred up conflict against the church in Kabul. Twice the church wall was attacked and damaged. In spite of efforts to negotiate, opposition hardened in official circles.

The acting mayor of Kabul sent the church an expropriation order in mid-1973.

Bulldozers and a demolition crew entered the compound on June 14. They crashed through the church walls and toppled the ceiling and roof. The equipment operators made every effort to smash the building into a pile of rubble. They even dug down under the foundation, searching for what they had been told was an underground church! Pastor J. Christy Wilson was traveling at that time. When he heard the news, he fell face down on the hotel carpet and let a tidal wave of grief crash over him.[4]

"Unless a kernel of wheat falls to the ground and dies, it remains only a single seed. But if it dies, it produces many seeds," Jesus said (John 12:24). As I write this, the season is autumn. Through many months, the maple tree outside my window has spread out its great, green, hand-shaped leaves. Last month they turned gold. Last week they dropped. The tree finally has let go of its huge sunny treasure. Now those tattered remnants lie rotting on the ground. The branches stretch out naked and somewhat ugly. The tree looks lifeless. But we who have lived through enough seasons know the truth of Jesus's words: death can prepare the way for a fresh onrush of life. When the only church building in Afghanistan was crushed, Pastor Wilson grieved. When the martyr Qazi Abdul Karim was commanded to renounce the Lord Jesus, he gave his life. Such sacrifices continue. But they are not wasted. Like the maple branches, they are packed with potential for the future.

So, while some Afghan believers die, others live for the Lord Jesus Christ. In this book we will meet Karim, a medical doctor. When his name went on a hit list, he rounded up his family and fled. Along the way they encountered the beauty and power of Jesus and became his followers. Rashid was an international student. To break up the hours at his desk, he went looking for a soccer scrimmage. He found one run by a local church. On the staff was an Iranian pastor who personally discussed the gospel with him over a period of months. Jesus became Rashid's Lord. Ahmad teaches the Gospels and the book of Acts to eighteen leaders-in-training inside Afghanistan. Through their quiet witness they have seen several small house fellowships take shape in 2022. Mariya runs an agency that serves refugees and immigrants in her city. Her motivation is her Lord Jesus Christ.

Is there hope for Afghanistan? Hebrews 11, the great "faith chapter," recounts the heroes of the faith—Abel, Enoch, Noah, Abraham, Isaac, Jacob,

---

4 Wilson, *Afghanistan*, 60.

Moses, Rahab, Gideon, Barak, Samson, Jephthah, David, Samuel, and the prophets. Some saw miracles. Some experienced amazing victories.

> Through faith [they] conquered kingdoms, administered justice, and gained what was promised. [They] shut the mouths of lions, quenched the fury of the flames, and escaped the edge of the sword; [their] weakness was turned into strength; and [they] became powerful in battle and routed foreign armies. Women received back their dead, raised to life again. (Heb 11:33–35)

This is what we pray for Afghans: wonderful breakthroughs, astounding spiritual support.

But the text does not stop there. It continues, and the tone grows far more somber and scary.

> There were others who were tortured, refusing to be released, so that they might gain an even better resurrection. Some faced jeers and flogging, and even chains and imprisonment. They were put to death by stoning; they were sawed in two; they were killed by the sword. They went about in sheepskins and goatskins, destitute, persecuted, and mistreated—the world was not worthy of them. They wandered in deserts and mountains, living in caves and in holes in the ground. (Heb 11:35–38)

Oh yes, this too is the Afghan experience. Regarding those who suffered, the text comments, "These were all commended for their faith, yet none of them received what had been promised … God had planned something better for us so that only together with us would they be made perfect" (Heb 11:39–40).

This is difficult and humbling reading. Is there hope for Afghanistan? God has plans, we are told. Better plans. Not only commendations for Afghans who were faithful in the past but also a vision for Afghans as part of a glorious multicultural future.

Martin Luther King said, "The arc of the moral universe is long, but it bends toward justice."[5] King's words echo the complexity of this text from Hebrews. King's optimism is not shared by all of our leading thinkers. Doomsday talk pops up regularly. Quite a few thoughtful people anticipate the human race flickering out because of our overuse of the earth's resources, our violent tendencies, and our increasingly powerful tools for destruction. In some circles there is a slight sense of mellow resignation in the air.

Where did Martin Luther King find the optimism for his conviction? King's hope erupted out of Jesus's resurrection. There will be crucifixions, yes. But beyond Jesus's cross explodes the resurrection. There is evil in this world, yes, but when evil has done its worst, here comes grace. In spite of all that has gone before, a way appears. Hope is reborn. Dreams are restored.

Even for Afghanistan.

---

5 Martin Luther King's Baccalaureate Address, Wesleyan University, 1964.

Mountain Faith

In that framework, this book envisions a future for Afghan people. We explore the geography and resources of the land. The colorful and challenging history, with multiple empires invading, but locals fiercely reasserting independence, then dissipating their power by fighting among themselves. Diverse languages, local economic patterns, music, poetry, celebrations, food. Political structures. Women's lives. Religion, especially Islam in its various expressions. International refugee journeys and settlements. Global Afghan connections.

Woven into this fabric are stories of Afghans who follow Jesus. Worshipping communities. Maturing disciples. Online churches. Media resources. Afghan praise music. Gospel bridges to Afghan worldviews. Marriage and child raising challenges and strategies. Microenterprise economic projects. Healthy multiethnic identities. Key celebrations.

Ways to help and bless Afghans, especially refugees, are detailed in this book. Specific resources and actions that can meet needs are cited. However, Afghans are not passive victims, but proud, capable people, with a significant heritage and also, by God's grace, a promising potential future. Is there hope for Afghanistan? The way ahead will not be easy. But resurrection life reverberates.

Afghanistan is the roof of the world. A wall of giants protrudes upward, from the Karakorum Mountains all the way through the Hindu Kush, Tien Shan, and Himalayan ranges. These include most of the highest precipices on earth. In just one range, the Pamir Knot, there are more than one hundred peaks higher than 20,000 feet. Only one mountain in the US is that high, Denali in Alaska. Think about the Rocky Mountains where a summit of 14,000 feet is considered remarkable—in Afghanistan's uplands, twenty-five pinnacles rise above 25,000 feet. These hulks are geologically active. Continental plates continue to jockey, and the Himalayas rise an inch every five years. Simultaneously, moving in the other direction, gravity gouges and carves the mountains by means of glaciers, rain, streams, and terrific winds.

Between Afghanistan and Pakistan, more than twenty-five passes cleave through sharp cliffs. Some of these routes can be hair-raising: one drivable pass has forty steep hairpin turns. On this approach, supply trucks load up with bags of grain or other ballasts in order to keep from sliding over the edges of the road. As the drivers chug upward, they also must swivel around avalanches, landslides, and fallen trees.

If the land is dangerous, so is worshipping Jesus in this nation. It demands tough faith, mountain faith, rugged, soaring, often scarred, but sinewy. Today Afghan Christians flourish in nearly thirty countries. Prayers to Jesus rise globally in Pashtu and Dari languages. But these believers still connect back home. Their faith, the faith of one people, is the subject of this volume.

This is a book about justice, about making vulnerable people our priority. This is a book about beauty, beautiful cultures in God's world and a beautiful global church. This is a book about relationships, because we are not born for small, self-centered lives: we are meant for greatness, walking with God to bless the peoples of the earth. This is a book about worship of the God who created diverse landforms and ecosystems and peoples. This is a book of lament. This is a book of practical strategies. This is a book of wisdom, with layers of meaning.

Since the church in Afghanistan was bulldozed in 1973, there has not been a single church building to serve the 40 million Afghans in that land. But the story is not finished.

Read on.

— CHAPTER 2 —

The God Who Comes Close

Flooding across America and Europe, Afghan refugees bring stories. But almost none of those stories are about an Afghan Christian. Those are rare jewels. Those never-before-recorded accounts are the sparkling stars in this chapter.

As we trace seekers' sincere questions, we find that our empathy is stirred. Glimpsing elements that drew Afghans to Christ stretches our understanding. Reflecting on these fresh journeys revitalizes our own personal walks.

Why do Afghans come to Jesus as Lord of the universe and Lord of their lives? Some come because they are gripped by a new vision of who God is. As Muslims, they already know that God is eternal, all-wise, all-powerful, the one who created everything and who will draw everything to a conclusion at the final judgment. God is "merciful and compassionate," in the words of their daily prayer. God blesses us with the gifts of nature and society. God cares about us enough to communicate with us through prophets and revelations. God notices us and records how we act. What we do matters. God has expectations for us.

But when Afghans migrate to Europe or North America, God often appears to be absent. God is not mentioned in school, and rarely in civic events. Most of the time he is missing from public life. Instead, people seem to worship material things and personal success.

Whatever Westerners may think, Afghans instinctively know that God is foundational to our lives. Yet many of them feel far away from God. "Earlier I felt only blackness," Abdul says. "I wanted to get closer to God. I felt his absence. I always thought God was angry with me, searching for my mistakes to punish me. There was no light in my life. That was my life in Islam."

Then Abdul met European and Iranian Christians who shared his high view of God. But they went further. God was not distant from them. God cared about every human being, no matter how insignificant. God even cared about Abdul. His friends gave him a Gospel of Luke, and he read it. Abdul "learned that God is searching for me. Here Jesus found me. God is not angry at me but sent his Son for me. Thank you, Lord, for so much you have given me. Peace reigns over my heart. I am here to be a witness, to say Jesus is my God, my Lord, and I worship Him with all my heart." Abdul was baptized in a church in Germany that is half Afghan and half Iranian.

Like Abdul, some Afghans come to Jesus as Lord when they get a new understanding of what God is like. So, one of them challenges his friends, "Pray and ask God: who are you?"[1]

Christians and Coffee

Sayed was a government official under President Karzai before the Taliban came to power. When Karzai left office, all his top men found it expedient to leave the country or at least get to the other end of the land, far away from the new government. Sayed had gained financially from his position, as was the custom. Now he realized that it was time to get out.

Sayed and his wife Aisha set off for Europe, intending to travel through Iran and Turkey. But Turkey's border was tightly guarded, and they could not get through. They waited and tried a second time. Again, Turkey turned them back. They huddled in makeshift lodgings in Iran, with money dwindling and Iranian police circling.

What to do?

"We'll have exit in the other direction, through Pakistan," Sayed told Aisha.

"But that means passing through the Taliban-controlled region of Afghanistan," she protested.

"Yes. But we have no more options. *Inshallah*, we'll get through. Drape yourself from head to foot, and don't say a word, because your Dari accent will be noticed."

They got into Pakistan. From there they traveled to Europe and settled down in Austria. They moved into government housing and eventually were granted asylum.

"Hey, they have free coffee at the Oasis center down the street," a friend told Sayed one day.

While Sayed was enjoying coffee, somebody gave him a Gospel of Luke in Farsi, the language of Iran. Farsi is close to Dari, Sayed's mother tongue.

---

1 Unless otherwise indicated, most of the contemporary life stories in this book were gathered through interviews conducted by Miriam Adeney, Rashid Aalish, Bob Silver, and Kathy Giske.

The Oasis center stocks Gospels in over fifty languages and makes them available as gifts for refugees.

Luke is a good choice for Muslims because it does not begin with strong statement about the deity of Christ, which can be a stumbling block for them.

Sayed took the Gospel home and set it on the coffee table in the living room. When Aisha saw it, she snatched it up. "You can't read that. You're a Muslim," she declared.

Aisha hid the book. But Sayed figured out where it was. He would take it out secretly, read it, then put it back.

Meanwhile, Aisha was curious. She also read the Gospel secretly. This went on for months. Sayed had a dream in which he saw the Bible and heard someone say, "Read this." Over time the words and acts of Jesus flowed into Sayed's and Aisha's awareness. Between readings, the wonderful stories and thoughts simmered just below the level of their consciousness. Now and then these ideas would surface to shed light on their current life and the choices and decisions they were facing. Then they would dive in and read some more.

Afghans treasure the Holy Scripture. Although the *Quran* is the most sacred, there are parts of the Old and New Testaments that are revered as having come from God, including the Torah, the Psalms, and the Gospels. Editors have corrupted these biblical books, they believe. Still, the writings are worthy of respect. Because of them, Jews and Christians are considered "people of the Book."

When Afghans are traveling on their journeys toward Jesus as Lord, the Bible usually plays a part. Seekers may read Gospels or Psalms, or hear Bible stories, or watch them on videos. Sayed and his wife read the book of Luke. In the end, both of them became believers. Jesus was their Lord, their touchstone, the empowering presence in this new life in a new land.

They began to volunteer at Oasis regularly. Sayed had a good command of English because he had worked with Americans in Kabul. A few months after he came to faith in Jesus, he met Bob, an American pastor who was taking a sabbatical in Austria and hung out at the Oasis. There were a lot of Afghan newcomers in the coffee bar. Four Afghans were hammering Sayed with questions about the Bible. Sayed turned to Bob, and asked, "If I translate, would you answer questions on the Bible?"

Eventually about fifteen Afghan men were standing around, soaking up Bible knowledge for forty-five minutes.

Sayed said, "We should do this every time the Oasis is open." After that, he would often get up and announce, "We will have a Bible question-answering time." Two or three times a week the group would go to another room and hash out the topic.

"I have no intention of converting, but I would like to know what you believe," one man said.

So the questions rolled out.

"Why did Jesus have to die?"

Bob began with Adam, sin, the need for sacrifice, and the Old Testament years of sacrifice. Muslims are familiar with that history of sacrifice.

"Is the Bible accurate? Hasn't it been changed?"

Bob answered, "Isn't Allah all-powerful? If Allah has given us the Bible, would he allow it to be corrupted? (As noted above, Muslims believe that significant parts of the Bible were given by Allah.) The Bible manuscripts date from before the Prophet Muhammad, and he had good things to say about the Bible (See *Quran* 5:71; 5:49, 52; 3:3; 10:94). The *Injeel* (the New Testament, especially the Gospels) is full of wonderful teaching that you do not want to miss. God cares for us and wants everybody to receive this good news."

"What's wrong with Islam?"

Bob answered, "Islam has no Savior. The Prophet Muhammad did not have the opportunity to read the *Injeel*, so he did not know what Jesus had really done. Also, Islam has a warrior heritage, and some Muslims have followed that example down to today, especially in Afghanistan. But Jesus gives a different example, the example of self-sacrificing love. This is something every country needs, including Afghanistan."

Sayed's language skills facilitated this interaction. After a year Sayed told Bob, "You don't need to do this anymore. I've heard all your answers lots of times. Now I can interact with the questions directly."

Bob had never met a Muslim before September 11, 2001. After the shocking disaster that day, he felt a strong impulse to learn about Islam. He got books and began to educate himself. Years later, when he and his wife took a three-month sabbatical, a missionary in Austria invited them to live in her house. From there Bob walked into the Oasis. Since his retirement, he has returned regularly. He loves to greet newcomers at the Oasis and learn their stories.

Sayed and Aisha are now members of a Farsi-speaking church in Austria.

One reason Afghans come to Christ is because of the care that Christians show them. Quite a few say, "It was the Christians who helped us. It was the Christians who were friendly. Not our Muslim brothers. Not the general society." Of course there are well-meaning, humanitarian citizens of any faith, or no faith, who help displaced people. Some create or participate in systems that tackle human need on a large scale. Others simply reach out as friendly neighbors. On the other hand, sadly, there are many Christians who ignore migrants and newcomers. In spite of all that, the care exhibited by Christians remains striking. Afghans come to Christ not just because of Bible truth or theological explanations, but also because real people demonstrate love. They live it out. Afghans have taken note of this. It draws them to Jesus Christ. Sometimes this starts with the aroma of coffee.

"I Will Kill Him!" A Transformed Life

Amir and Yaqub had been friends for many years. Both of them lived in Turkey. Their friendship was precious to them. What a pleasure it was to drop in at each other's homes in the evenings, sit down, relax, drink coffee, eat snacks, gossip, joke, complain, wrestle over issues, and speculate about the future. In a life that held so much insecurity, what a blessing it was to have a sure friend.

But the friendship broke apart. Amir borrowed Yaqub's car, and wrecked it. The wreck happened because the brakes failed.

"It wasn't my fault!" Amir protested. "Yaqub should have maintained the car. Why, anybody could have been killed. Thank God, it was only the vehicle that was lost."

"Only the vehicle!" Yaqub roared. "Only the vehicle! It was *my* car that was destroyed. And Amir was driving. He should have noticed when the brakes got soft. To be honest, I hesitated about loaning the car to him, because I know that he's an irresponsible driver. He pushes too hard through the traffic and takes chances. He wouldn't bother to pay attention to any problem inside the car. And now—now I have no way to get to my job. Where will I find the funds for a replacement car? Amir must pay."

"Oh, I must pay?" Amir roared back. "I must buy Yaqub a new car to replace his defective one? No way. I will contribute, of course, to mitigate the hardship. But really, the bulk of the fault is his."

"I will kill him!" Yaqub shouted. "Not only has he taken my car, but he has insulted and defamed me. I will never visit his house again. And if our paths cross, be warned. I will not be responsible for my actions."

"Nor will I!" Amir retorted. "I can wield a knife as well as he can."

The two friends became bitter enemies. Both of them vowed revenge to the death.

Months passed. They managed to keep apart. Eventually Amir moved to another area of the city for work and family reasons. In his new neighborhood were some Iranians. Since they were congenial and spoke a language similar to his, he began to spend time with them.

Amazingly, some of the Iranians were followers of Jesus the Messiah, whom they called Jesus the Lord.

"Would you like to join us at a conference?" they invited Amir one day. "You're always trying to make sense of what we believe. This conference will be four days, and you'll really get the message."

"Why not?" Amir thought. He admired the pleasant spirit of his Jesus-following friends. Maybe there would be something he could learn.

That was an understatement. At the conference, Amir discovered that God cared so much for people that he himself—the God of all creation—adopted human form in the person of the prophet Jesus. He lowered himself even to the point of experiencing human death. In Jesus God himself became a sacrifice for us. But death could not hold him. Jesus rose right out of the grave, generating power for new beginnings. Some of that power is available to us when we submit to the Lord Jesus Christ.

Amir became a Jesus-follower. He joined his friends in worship and thanks and adoration, and also in heartfelt and honest pleas to God for help when he had problems. With his friends he began to understand the lessons of the *Injeel*, the Gospels, as well as the Torah of Moses and the *Zabur* or psalms of David. He learned what God offers us and what God expects, and he began to internalize daily disciplines of the Christian life.

At the conference, one teaching had riveted Amir. On the cross, Jesus said, "Father, forgive them." He said it to men who were murdering him!

How could the prophet Jesus forgive those men? Amir wondered. Over the days and weeks that followed, this paradoxical saying stuck like a stone in his shoe. It bothered him. He couldn't forget it. "Forgive them." This could only be the love of God, something supernatural.

Such love extended to Amir, too. God had accepted him. Now if he wanted to be godly, if he wanted to follow in the steps of Jesus, was he required to forgive? Never! Unthinkable! That was too much to expect of any man.

But was it too much to expect of the Spirit of God? And the Spirit of God lived inside Amir now. His co-workers commented that he was different. So did his neighbors. He demonstrated more patience in listening, more readiness to help, more joyful smiles.

The day came when Amir crossed the city and made his way to Yaqub's house, a place where he had enjoyed so many coffees but now had abandoned because of his great anger. Yaqub's wife opened the door. She stared at him in horror. Then with all her strength she slammed the door shut.

"Please open the door. I come in peace," Amir called.

"Let him come in! I'm ready," Yaqub yelled from the back room. When the wife opened the door again and fearfully let Amir in, Yaqub was coming forward with a weapon in his hand.

Quickly Amir said, "Before you kill me, I have something to tell you." He told the amazing story of God in Jesus, and of the changes in his own life. "Jesus said, 'Father, forgive them.' That's why I've come."

Yaqub and his wife were amazed. "We want to hear more," they said. One week later they themselves became committed followers of Jesus. They had seen an Afghan who was transformed by the love of God, and this drew them to the Lord Jesus Christ.

Dreams and Visions

Like Jacob in the Old Testament and Peter and Cornelius in the New Testament, many Afghans have dreams or visions with spiritual significance. Jared, for example, had been given a Gospel, and had read it. Then one night he had a dream. In his dream, a vast crowd was moving toward Mecca. But there was a chasm in front of them. One by one, people were falling down into the crevice. Jared tried to reverse direction, but he could not. Instead, he was being pushed inexorably forward toward the abyss.

He cried out, "Jesus! Save me!"

An angel came down and pulled him out of the crowd to safety.

When he woke up, he gave his life to Christ.

Another Afghan, Abdura had heard the gospel but was not willing to believe. He had a series of dreams. In one, he was digging a grave. There was a body already in it. The body came alive, and another body was put in its place. Then Abdura felt the truth that Jesus had died for him, that Jesus's body had been substituted for Abdura's.

The next night Abdura saw a light and heard a voice saying, "Your heart should wake up."

It did. That week he approached Sayed in the Oasis center, and asked, "How do I turn my life over to Christ?"

Still another Afghan, Farid was born into a semi-religious family. At the age of eighteen he emigrated out of Afghanistan toward a better life somewhere else. For a while he lived in Iran. There he began to explore religions, including Zoroastrianism and Christianity. An Armenian friend invited him to church. Social and political strictures kept Farid from attending church, but he did hear about Jesus because an Iranian friend and his father always were talking about the Lord. When Farid said goodbye to his friends as he moved on to Europe, he requested, "Pray for me."

In Europe Farid fell into vices and sins, and soon his life was a tangle of problems. He felt very alone. But his conscience kept prodding him. One day he felt a hand on his shoulder. Who was it? There was no one there. Was Jesus coming to him because of his friends' prayers?

Later he had a dream. Many people were walking toward a light. Farid turned around and went in the opposite direction. On his way, he stumbled into a marsh. He struggled to get out, but only succeeded in getting sucked down further. He realized that he could not save himself. Then he saw Jesus.

"Lord, help me!" Farid called.

"Come out!" Jesus answered.

Farid tried, but he could not extricate himself. Finally he grabbed Jesus's robe and held on until he was pulled free from the muck.

"When I woke up, I told Jesus I would follow Him the rest of my life," Farid testified. "I'm here to declare that Jesus is my Lord, my Savior, and my king."

One more Afghan, Zarif was born in a practicing Muslim family, but he had questions and doubts. He looked for answers. Who is God? Is my religion correct? He heard a little about Jesus and met some believers. Those people seemed to lack hatred. Nor were they scared of God. Instead, they emanated love. Zarif wanted to be like that—to experience love so that he could love others too.

"I always knew it was not just the name Allah that mattered, but that there was someone who was protecting me. I was given a lot of signs and evidences that I needed to choose the right way," Zarif says.

By 2015 Zarif had emigrated and was living abroad. It was time to clarify things. He had been taught that it was wrong to study other faiths, but he felt a need to find out who God is, and now he had the freedom to pursue it. Zarif prayed, then sought out a friend named Laila who knew about *Isa* (Jesus). "Help me sort this out," Zarif said to her.

"Okay," Laila said. "Let's set up some regular lessons about the Holy Scriptures."

They met in a coffee shop. When they began to read the Bible, Zarif remembers, "Something started to mess with me very strongly. I began to see horrible pictures and couldn't look at my friend. I saw people around with ugly, bloody faces, like human monsters. I wanted to run from the table. I felt like I had high blood pressure and was physically weak. I had a strong desire to fight with my friend and leave."

She saw that Zarif was disturbed.

But during all of this, Zarif was praying in the name of Jesus, about whom they had been talking. "I realized this opposition was from Satan," Zarif remembers. "I had to make a decision about whether he would win over me. I thought: If this opposition comes from Satan, then the right way is in front of me."

Zarif turned to his friend. "Please pray for me!" he pled. Then he asked Jesus to set him free. If Jesus was God, He could free Zarif from this demonic influence.

He looked at his friend, and at the people around, and realized that the ugly images had all disappeared. Then the desire welled up to know more of these stories of Jesus.

After the third lesson, Zarif felt that he was beginning to understand the books of the Torah that they were studying. "I saw a God who wants to communicate with me. He is alive and loving. I saw that God wants to reveal himself, but there may be spiritual oppression from Satan. I know I need to continue to open my heart to *Isa al-Masih* (Jesus the Messiah) and his truth. Satan will fight but we must hold on and continue on God's path versus the path of Islam."

Justice and Women

There is a powerful story recorded in John 8. A group of religious leaders shoved a woman forward to stand in front of Jesus.

> The teachers of the law and the Pharisees brought in a woman caught in adultery. They made her stand before the group and said to Jesus, "Teacher, this woman was caught in the act of adultery. In the Law Moses commanded us to stone such women. Now what do you say?" They were using this question as a trap, in order to have a basis for accusing him. (John 8:3–6)

In Afghanistan, during periods when the strictest fundamentalists are in power, women like this woman in John 8 are killed. Though many Afghans deplore cruel punishment, Navid Hamdi, an Afghan executive in Seattle, did witness just such a woman's execution during half time at a soccer match in 2022.

What would Jesus say? He loved the law of God. Would he approve carrying out the punishment that was mandated?

> When they kept on questioning him, he straightened up and said to them, "Let any one of you who is without sin be the first to throw a stone at her." Again he stooped down and wrote on the ground.
>
> At this, those who heard began to go away one at a time, the older ones first, until only Jesus was left, with the woman still standing there. Jesus straightened up and asked her, "Woman, where are they? Has no one condemned you?"
>
> "No one, sir," she said.
>
> "Then neither do I condemn you," Jesus declared. "Go now, and leave your life of sin." (John 8:7–11)

Several Afghan men have observed that the way women are portrayed in the Gospels provides a good model. Two men testified when they were baptized, "This is the gospel story that strikes me most powerfully. When I read it, I knew I must follow Jesus."

While some Afghan women enjoy caring relationships and creative outlets, many suffer. Particularly under the Taliban they endure crippling restrictions, such as the end of schooling for teenage girls. Both inside and outside the country, people cling to the hope that eventually there will be a more just society. If women are half the population, equity has to include fair treatment for them. Jesus's affirmation, forgiveness, and restoration of women is one more reason Afghans are drawn to him.

Love Casts Out Fear

Rashid was not even three years old when his family had to flee. Instead of batting at stones in the courtyard, then popping into the house for a snack, he was grabbed by his mother's hand and hustled to the car. The Russian-backed government was collapsing. Civil war was breaking out. *Mujahideen*—soldiers of religious armies—invaded towns. Massacres stained the soil. Young men were conscripted against their will. Women were not safe. This was especially true for people in Rashid's ethnic group, the Hazara. It was time to leave.

Although they were not rich, Rashid's family had enjoyed food, friends, and festivities. Now they abandoned everything and scurried through deserts into the foreign land of Iran. Here they were not welcome. They were viewed as just one more bunch of refugees squeezing in. Still, the Iranians could put them to work.

"I have a job on a construction crew," Rashid's father announced.

"And I've found work as a maid," his mother reported.

What relief: at least the five children would eat. Also they could go to school. However, when it came to worship, the family had to pray secretly, or they would get into trouble. In school and in public, they had to practice mainstream Shia Islam alongside the Iranians. Yet Rashid's family were Ismaili Muslims and had their own traditions which they considered essential.

As he grew up, little Rashid would wonder, "What really is the right way to worship? Who is God? How can we know Him?" He was curious. But he heard no answers.

When he was fifteen, the family dropped some bad news on him. "You're going to have to stop school, Rashid. Your father's asthma is worse. He can't hold a job anymore. Since Abdul (Rashid's older brother) is married with little children, he has to support his own family. It's up to you now."

For two years Rashid worked to support the family. Then he was able to return to school, working only in the summers. He was a good student and was just about to graduate from high school when his hopes were crushed: the Iranian government announced that Afghan refugees would no longer be allowed to study in public or private schools.

Most of Rashid's classmates dropped out of school and got jobs. But his family wanted something more. In 2003 they moved back to Afghanistan, where Rashid and his sisters could continue to go to school.

Meanwhile, the first Taliban regime had collapsed. A new government was in place. Although there were not many jobs, Rashid's father had inherited a house with a little land where he began to raise a few calves. That worried Rashid. He loved education. Yet if he failed the university matriculation exam, he would be doomed to join his father as a farmer for the rest of his life.

Thank God, he passed the exam! God was watching over him, though Rashid didn't know it then. But he did continue to wonder about God. Even though he was back in his home country, he often had to hide his own Ismaili religious practices. Outwardly he had to conform to the majority Afghan tradition, which was Sunni Islam. It was confusing.

Rashid decided to dig deeper to try to understand Islam. He ended up with a lot of questions. When he gave voice to them in class, controversies erupted. His professors got angry with him for raising such issues. Although it was against the rules, they suspended him for a year. Because Rashid valued education, he decided to keep quiet when he came back to school.

After graduating from university, Rashid won a year-long study trip to the US. This opened his eyes to a bigger world. He observed how freely people chose their religion and way of life. He noticed the ways that different ethnicities and nationalities mingled together and co-existed. By contrast, Rashid himself felt overloaded with religious obligations. Although he was not breaking any Muslim rules, he worried that he was not accomplishing enough to satisfy God and access God's grace in this world. What was the truth, anyway?

For a while Rashid decided to quit fretting about what specific Islamic sect people followed. He simply focused on God as the source of grace. What was the point of disputing with his fellow Afghans about which prophet was better? With his ongoing sense of curiosity, Rashid still had more questions than answers. However, he knew if he asked those questions aloud he might be accused of insulting Islam.

Then God blessed Rashid with another scholarship to study in the US, this time for a graduate degree. When he remembered having to leave school earlier, he was amazed. It seemed unbelievable. As he progressed with his study, however, the old questions would not stay quiet. Fear and frustration began to fester.

Among his friends was a woman named Lois. One day, after he had voiced some of his religious perplexity, she asked, "Would you like to read the Bible? Here, take mine."

At first Rashid thought it would be a sin to read the Bible. But nobody else would know if he had a Bible in his room. So he took it, and, as was his habit when he first opened a book, he skipped around to several spots. One passage caught his eye: 1 John 4:7–21.

Three ideas in this passage impacted him. First, God is love and love is God. What an amazing description of God!

Second, God sent Jesus to save us, and if we acknowledge that Jesus is the Son of God, God will live in us and we will live in God.

Third, there is no fear in love, but perfect love drives out fear.

Rashid had been feeling quite a lot of worry, frustration, and disappointment about the future. He feared that sooner or later God would punish him. This biblical text made a deep impression on him. Rashid and Lois began to discuss different Bible passages. The uniqueness of Christianity was emerging.

Then Rashid met Sepehr. Wherever Rashid had lived, whether in Afghanistan, Iran, or the US, he always had loved to play soccer. Now as a graduate student who needed to get away from the library occasionally, Rashid had wondered: Is there any pick-up soccer team here that I could join?

"Yes, there's a team that plays right through the winter on an indoor field on Queen Anne Hill," he was told.

"Great!" he thought.

"It's in the gym of the First Free Methodist Church."

"What?!" As a Muslim, he believed it was a sin to go to any church activity. But—wait! He was in America. Maybe he could relax the rules for a good cause, the game of soccer. So he joined the scrimmage and got regular workouts.

That was where he met Sepehr, a young Iranian man who was on the church's pastoral staff. Their Dari and Farsi languages were similar. A friendship began to develop. When soccer season ended, Rashid decided to ask Sepehr a couple of questions. Sepehr was welcoming, Rashid felt comfortable with him, and soon their conversations were lasting for hours.

As a Muslim, Rashid knew that he was supposed to pray five times a day, fast during the month of Ramadan, donate an annual *zakat* contribution, eventually make a pilgrimage to Mecca in Arabia, and meanwhile think constantly about how to please God. Through these good works he hoped that ultimately he would be among God's chosen ones. Yet it was not clear whether, at the end of all his efforts, he would make it to heaven or not.

By contrast, Rashid learned, the Christian faith teaches that God himself knew we would not be able to save ourselves. Therefore, God was willing to step into this world to die for us and become our Savior. This is not a God who stands back and watches us suffer—this is a God who takes action, steps off his throne, and says to the angels who worship God constantly, "I am coming into the world as a baby."

How could God be born and become a baby in this world? Never had Rashid considered this possibility. He had always thought of God just as the

Quran had presented him. It was challenging to envision any other reality. So Rashid delved into both the *Quran* and the Bible. What he found surprised him. The *Quran* seemed to confirm some of what the New Testament was saying about Jesus Christ!

Rashid found: (1) the name of Jesus is in twenty-five places in the *Quran*, while he could only see the name of Muhammad in four places; (2) the *Quran* mentions no woman by name except Mary, for whom there is a chapter named; (3) chapter 3:34 and following verses say that Mary was born without original sin, she never committed any sin in her life, she was ever a virgin, and she went to heaven with her physical body; (4) chapter 3:44–55 describes Jesus as (a) *Kalimatullah*, which means Word of God; (b) *Rohullah*, which means Spirit of God; and (c) *Isa Masih*, which refers to Jesus Christ as Messiah; this passage also says Jesus (d) spoke when he was two days old; (e) created a live bird out of mud, which means that he could give life; (f) cured blindness and leprosy; and (g) went to heaven while he was still alive, and will come back.

Rashid compared these *Quranic* verses with the Bible. He knew that John 1 says that the Word is God, and that God is one being in three persons: God, Jesus Christ, and the Holy Spirit. He realized that there is no verse in the *Quran* that describes Muhammad doing miracles. He remembered that Muhammad married eleven wives, while Jesus did not marry at all.

The more Rashid read, the more he discovered that he had been pursuing the wrong route to reach God. This disconnection had placed him in a crisis situation. He had felt afraid, disappointed, and frustrated because he was unable to satisfy Allah's requirements and access his grace. Rashid realized that God is the source of eternal love for humans; that whoever accepts that Jesus Christ is the Son of God and the only reliable Savior in this world, will live in God and God will live in them. He realized that there is no fear in love, because perfect love drives out fear.

Sepehr helped a lot. As Rashid read the Bible and talked to Sepehr, he began to come out of his crisis. He felt like he was being born again. His fear, frustration, disappointment, and pessimism about the future were disappearing. After several months of curiosity, exploration, and realization, Rashid decided that he was ready to accept Christianity as his religion. He went to Sepehr and told him that he was ready to come to faith.

So Sepehr read the testimony and Rashid repeated it, testifying to his acceptance of the Father, Son, and Holy Spirit.

Intriguingly, on the very day when Rashid was going to meet Sepehr, a woman stopped him on the street. He was wearing headphones so this interruption was unusual. Rashid thought she was lost. But instead she asked him, "Would you like to learn about Jesus Christ?"

For some moments he was so surprised that he could not breathe. Then he told her his story. She invited him to come to her Bible study classes. After he accepted the faith, he did attend those classes, which were held at the First Free Methodist Church. Providentially he found a very kind, generous, and welcoming congregation there. He never felt like an outsider when he was with them.

Baptism, Rashid learned, is a rite of admission and adoption, and a sign of new birth. Rashid wanted to be baptized to obey Jesus Christ, to express his belief in a crucified, buried, and risen Savior, to start a new life by burying his old one, and to be born again and live in newness of life in Jesus Christ. He talked to the lead pastor of the First Free Methodist Church. Around Easter, Rashid was baptized. Subsequently he became a member of the church. When he was baptized, Rashid says, he felt relieved of the crisis that had put him under stress, fear, frustration, and disappointment, and the constant feeling that God would punish him because he was not a good servant. His heart opened to the greatness of God who is love, eternal love. Baptism also gave Rashid the opportunity to declare himself publicly as a Christian with a commitment to God, Jesus Christ, and the Holy Spirit.

God is great and does amazing things in the lives of his people. God had a plan for Rashid and put him on a journey to explore and search for the truth. Although he went through difficult times with many ups and downs, Rashid was blessed by the will of God and finally found Jesus Christ.

While Afghanistan may be the hardest country in the world in which to be a Christian, that does not stop Afghans like Sayed, Amir, Yaqub, Abdura, Farid, Zarif, and Rashid from experiencing the grace of God in Jesus. Each story, each journey, each person is unique and valued by the God who made each one.

However, they have not been dropped into this world as lone individuals. They also belong to a community. What is this heritage? What is the context that has shaped them? The next four chapters will explore the land and its resources. Social patterns between men and women. Government, including the Taliban. Religion, especially Islam. Then comes a chapter on the great upheaval of refugees. Finally, three chapters will probe details of Afghan Christian life today, details that have never been published before.

— Chapter 3 —

Begin with the Land

How do physical resources shape our lives? Four chapters explore Afghan culture—patterns of material things, family, politics, and religion. This chapter focuses on the land and its resources, including rural sheep herders, urban centers and international trade ties, farm villages and their community relationships and values, and biblical themes, beginning with the motif of the shepherd and ending with the mandate to care for God's creation.

Two World Trade Center towers collapsed in New York City. Americans stared at their screens in disbelief. Meanwhile a plane full of ordinary travelers arrowed through the sky, oblivious to the disaster below. Some passengers watched movies, others played games, slept, or gazed idly at the cotton-ball clouds.

Suddenly hijackers unclicked their seat belts, erupted into the aisles, brandished weapons, wrested control of the plane, and pointed it in a new direction.

Todd Beamer was on that plane. A graduate of Wheaton College and a devout Christian, he stared at the terrorists in shock. Then, little by little, he and several other passengers began to access current news on their phones. The happenings in New York were unbelievable. But what was happening on their own plane? There was no question that it had changed direction. It seemed to be heading toward Washington DC. Why? Was it aiming for the White House? Or the Pentagon?

Not on our watch, they communicated covertly to each other. *We will not be a passive part of any destruction like that.* Silently they crafted a rough plan. When it was ready, they acted.

"Let's roll!" Beamer shouted.

Jumping up, the passengers tackled the terrorists. The plane crashed. Everyone on board was killed. However, this heroic move saved many more lives on the ground in the nation's capital.

Before Beamer shouted, he softly recited a prayer, then continued with Psalm 23:

> The Lord is my shepherd. I lack nothing.
> He makes me lie down in green pastures,
> He leads me beside quiet waters,
> He restores my soul.
> He guides me along the right paths for his name's sake.
> Even though I walk through the darkest valley, I will fear no evil
> For You are with me.
> Your rod and your staff, they comfort me.
> You prepare a table before me in the presence of my enemies.
> You anoint my head with oil. My cup overflows.
> Surely your goodness and love will follow me all the days of my life,
> And I will dwell in the house of the Lord forever.

For three thousand years this Psalm has been known and loved by all kinds of people. The shepherd motif in the Bible reaches across time and space, touching people as different as Todd Beamer in a crashing plane in the United States and the sheep-herding nomads of Afghanistan.

Afghan Shepherds and Biblical Shepherds

Herding always has been a pivotal occupation in Afghanistan. With their flocks and herds—fat-tailed sheep for meat and karakul sheep for wool—nomads have roamed far and wide. Though their earnings are not a big part of the national economy, the free-roaming herder represents an ideal. He is tough, competent, self-supporting and self-sufficient, a master of nature and of his own fate.

If we want to understand a people, we must begin with their land, with their material and economic resource base. God has created us physical beings and placed us in a sensory world. Land influences the possibilities of our lives. A desert people will differ from an ocean people, an arctic people will contrast with a jungle people. For any society, the land and its resources will carve and channel the options available to them, not only limiting their 1) food and work but also influencing their 2) family and political patterns, and 3) and values and ideals. To learn about a people, we begin with the land. In Afghanistan that means beginning with shepherds and herders.

Traditionally, herders' and shepherds' families have accompanied their animals on regular migration routes, up into the mountains for forage in the summer and back down into the valleys for shelter in the winter. The highest pastures top out at fifteen thousand feet above sea level. Sheep, goats, camels, donkeys, and horses all may be part of the moving menagerie. Small children and even baby animals are tied onto the larger animals, along with tents, poles, containers of kerosene, wood, and leather packing cases. Today trucks often replace camels on these travels.

When the people are on foot or riding animals, scouts roam between migrating groups. Boys and sheep and goats skip over high trails, while elders and families with children move along on parallel lower trails. The rate of travel is slow, no more than fifteen miles a day.

Upon arriving at a campsite—often a regular, well-known rest spot—the women set up their family tents and cook supper, while the men corral the animals.

Occasionally they will pass near communities of settled people or isolated farmer's homesteads. Sometimes there is conflict but at other times the shepherds' and herders' relationship with these settled people is symbiotic. Manure from their animals fertilizes the farmers' fields. The migrants' information networks bring fresh news to local communities. Wealthier herders may even serve as moneylenders to farmers who have a need for extra cash. Some nomads collect annual rents from those who owe them money when they pass through the farmers' lands.

Like migrant herders and shepherds worldwide, these nomads do not own their grazing grounds. In the United States, for example, cattle ranchers often arrange to use public lands like national forests for their summer grazing. Traditionally, Afghans' migration routes extended into what is now Pakistan. British colonial rulers drew a border between the two nations. Called the Durand Line, this cuts right through the heartland of the Pashtun people. Citizens on both sides of the border continue to feel connected, tied in a way that transcends this artificial barrier. Herders in particular would like to proceed on their normal routes and access their customary grazing lands. Increasingly, however, they feel constrained to stay within Afghanistan. The danger of crossing the border with all their animals outweighs the benefits.

Back home, other dangers loom. While the herdsmen are in the mountains, farmers may move onto their traditional winter grounds in the valleys. Upon returning in the fall, the nomads may discover that they have lost access to the places where they normally sheltered their animals during the cold season. For a variety of reasons, some herders become semi-sedentary. They exchange their goat-hair or camel-hair tents for mud huts. Part of the group will continue to migrate with the flocks and herds, while the rest will settle down and raise crops. Still, they treasure their identity as nomads.

In the Bible are hundreds of references to sheep and shepherds. Even God takes the title of Shepherd for himself (Ps 78:52). Moses and David are called shepherds of the people (Isa 63:11; Ps 78:70). Isaiah compares human beings to wandering sheep: "We all, like sheep, have gone astray" (Isa 53:6). Isaiah also pictures the ultimate Good Shepherd: "He tends his flock like a shepherd. He gathers the lambs in his arms and carries them close to his heart; he gently leads those that have young" (Isa 40:11).

Jesus describes a flock with one hundred sheep. Ninety-nine of those sheep return to the fold, but one is missing. The shepherd goes out into the scrub and searches. When the sheep finally is found, joy percolates throughout the community (Luke 15). On another occasion, Jesus calls himself the "Good Shepherd" who protects his sheep, going so far as to give his life for them (John 10).

Both Paul and Peter call for Christian leaders to be shepherds (Acts 20; 1 Peter 5). Peter lays out detailed guidelines:

> Be shepherds of God's flock that is under your care, watching over them—
> not because you must, but because you are willing, as God wants you to be,
> not pursuing dishonest gain, but eager to serve, not lording it over those
> entrusted to you, but being examples to the flock. And when the Chief
> Shepherd appears, you will receive the crown of glory that will never fade
> away. (1 Pet 5:2–4)

In Afghanistan it is not only migrant herders who value sheep and goats. Even a settled traditional family will benefit from access to such animals. Clothes and tents are woven from the fibers of the coat. Milk, cheese, butter, and yogurt yield daily protein. Festivals, parties, celebrations and unexpected guests are possible because you can always roast a goat or sheep. Carpets, one of the glories of Afghanistan, are fashioned from goat hair and sheep's wool. Goats in particular are tough. They can forage on all sorts of scrub. And they are mobile—if you need to move, your animals move with you. And if you need vegetables or tea or sugar or matches or even guns or ammunition, you can sell or trade some animals.

The shepherd motif that is so pervasive in the Bible is a theme that Afghans can resonate with. Their shepherds may be unpolished, but they are proud of their competence. They know how to negotiate long arcs of migration. They are superb in coping with unexpected difficulties along the way. They live in harmony with nature. To a significant extent, they are free men. When things are going well, the nomad life feels like the best life in the world.

Cities, Palaces, Bazaars

Most Afghans are not nomads, however. Traditionally, most have been farmers, tradesmen, or merchants, cultivating the land, crafting products, and distributing the produce. Yet farmsteads and simple villages have not been as isolated as one might suppose. Although this land lies deep in the mountains of Central Asia and might seem almost inaccessible, multiple powerful civilizations have flowed over it. Rarely has the region of Afghanistan been left alone.

The mountain routes and passes of this region "were already old when the Silk Route caravans were young, bringing exotic goods, people, and beliefs into some of the region's remotest areas." The extent of this trade is epitomized by "the royal blue lapis lazuli found in 5,000-year-old Sumerian tombs and inlaid into the 3,000-year-old gold mummy case of the ancient Egyptian King Tutankhamen. [This lapis lazuli] comes only from a single high mountain mine in Badakshan."[1]

When Alexander the Great passed through Afghanistan, he introduced elements of Greek civilization. Even earlier, Cyrus' empire had sprinkled aspects of Persian culture across the land. Later, when Buddhism moved from India to China during the period from the third to the sixth centuries, the missionary monks made the journey by means of a route through the Afghan mountain passes. Pausing in the remote Bamiyan Valley, they built a massive monastic complex and carved out the world's tallest Buddhas.

During the following centuries, Mongol and Indian cultures arrived, spearheaded by renowned leaders like Timur and Babur. Christian missionaries, too, journeyed along the Silk Road from Iran and Syria. They joined native Afghans who had been following Jesus ever since they heard Peter's sermon at the feast of Pentecost recorded in Acts 2.

With these complex civilizational exchanges, and with Afghanistan's own rich agricultural, mineral, and gem resources, some of its settlements shimmered into remarkably opulent displays. Balkh, also known as Bactria, one of the earliest great cities of Afghanistan, was known for its gardens of oranges, grapes, almonds, pomegranates, lilies, sugar cane, and turmeric. Besides the formidable city wall and efficient water supply system, it boasted finely crafted gold objects displaying miniature horses and carriages and humans. These delicate art pieces have been dated as early as the fifth century BC.[2]

Archaeological excavations in the twentieth and twenty-first centuries have unearthed treasures of gold, silver, bronze, copper, tin, lead, turquoise, and lapis lazuli, as well as pottery, carved wooden objects, and Chinese porcelain. The Oxus Treasure alone has yielded 180 items of gold and silver. These are guarded by the National Museum of Afghanistan. (Whenever it becomes necessary, as during times of war and violence, the museum staff has learned how to hide valuable historic items, although inevitably a good deal has been lost.)

---

1 Barfield, *Afghanistan*, 46.

2 Simpson, *Afghanistan*, 33–38, 98–101.

The Indian ruler Babur (1483–1530) extolled Afghanistan in his memoir *Baburnama*. He writes: "Down to Kabul every year come seven, eight, or ten thousand horses, and up to it, from Hindustan, come every year caravans of ten, fifteen, twenty thousand heads of houses, bringing slaves, white cloth, sugar candy, refined and common sugars, and aromatic roots. ... In Kabul can be had the products of Khurasan, Rum (Turkey), Iran, and China, while it is Hindustan's own market."[3]

Afghanistan's biggest expansion was achieved in the 1700s under Ahmad Shah, ruler of the Durrani Empire. When he died in 1772, the empire included all of today's Afghanistan, Baluchistan (in Pakistan), Korasan (in Iran), and the former Mughal territories of Sind and Punjab (in Pakistan) and Kashmir. Unfortunately, the state began to unravel in the next generation.[4]

Contributing to this unraveling were the diverse ethnic peoples of the region. They surrounded and observed the luxury of whatever central government was in power. Naturally the wealth of the cities was a temptation. Periodically this would give rise to attacks from militarily strong desert societies, especially camel Bedouins and horse-riding Turks, or fiercely independent mountain peoples. Central governments might flourish for a time, but when the people on the margins sensed an opportunity, they would charge in. Ironically, however, as a Chinese proverb attests, "While an empire can be won on horseback, it cannot be ruled from there."[5]

Tensions between the center and the periphery have a long history here. In 1809, British legate Mountstuart Elphinstone commented, "The internal government of the tribes answers its end so well that the utmost disorders of the royal government never derail its operations, nor disturb the lives of the people. A number of organized and high-spirited republics are ready to defend their rugged country against a tyrant." He quotes an Afghan: "We are content with discord, we are content with alarms, we are content with blood, we will never be content with a master."[6]

Even today chasms continue to yawn between the slightly modern cities and the rural regions, between the official national government and informal local bodies, between mountain and valley peoples, between Sunnis, Shiites, Ismailis, and spiritists, between those who speak Pashtu and those who prefer Dari or another language, and between those of different political persuasions.

Modernization began after World War II. During the Soviet period of the 1980s, it continued with a communist flavor, and sped up under the

---

3 Simpson, *Afghanistan*, 130.
4 Dupree, *Afghanistan*, 334.
5 Barfield, *Afghanistan*, 88.
6 Simpson, *Afghanistan*, 135.

influence of Americans from 2002–2021. Although Afghanistan is one of the least urban countries, Kabul now has five million inhabitants. Several million Afghans have returned from abroad, bringing entrepreneurial skills as well as funds to invest in small businesses. In Kabul the Taliban government has 180 projects underway to provide utility services, build major roads, plant trees, and improve neglected areas. Similar projects are rolling out in other major cities. Some of these improvements were outlined in a master plan created by President Mohammed Daoud Khan forty-three years ago. Taxes and fees and international donors are to pay for the projects.

Today Afghanistan has four major regions, each identified by a city: Kabul in the east; Qandahar in the south; Herat in the west; and Mazar-I Sharif in the north. There is also "Afghanistan's phantom limb," the Northwest Frontier Province of Pakistan anchored in the city of Peshawar. Millions of Pashtuns reside in this province. Many believe it should still be part of Afghanistan.

Life at the Local Level

Settled farmers have formed the backbone of the economy throughout time. To be sure, not all the land is suitable for farming. Dozens of jagged, snow-covered mountain ranges extend out from the Himalayas. The south of the country features vast, desert-like areas, and other places are swamps. All in all, it is estimated that only 12 percent of the land area is cultivable.

In spite of the forbidding terrain, wheat flourishes in the valleys. Some scholars believe that Afghanistan is the first place wheat was grown as a crop. Other grains and vegetables thrive here also. In the lowlands, it is common to see cotton, melons, and citrus fruits. In the highlands, mulberries and nuts abound.

Tragically, the most lucrative crop is represented by the white poppies swaying in the fields. Opium poppies are drought-tolerant. They do not rot on long trading trips. And a farmer can earn almost twenty times more by growing poppies than he can earn by growing wheat.

There is a long history of poppy-growing in the Afghan region, but it expanded in a major way in the 1950s when the neighboring country of Iran banned the crop. In the 1980s it expanded again. At that time the Afghans were battling the Soviets who had invaded. To finance their resistance, warlords increased their poppy harvests. Since then, there have been booms and bans, depending on the policies and priorities of the government in power.

In recent years it has been estimated that as much as 90 percent of the illegal heroin distributed globally originates in Afghanistan. Overall, the crop provides roughly four hundred thousand jobs for farmers, warlords, government officials, and traffickers. This commercialization of agriculture at a new level has transformed a subsistence crop structure into an export economy, resulting in a massive transfer of wealth.[7]

In April 2022 the Taliban outlawed the crop again, right during the poppy harvest. In 2023 the government's eradication of poppies increased markedly. Whether this will have much long-term effect on the quantity of opium produced and exported remains to be seen. In the short term, small farmers whose fields are destroyed are devastated. They talk about having to sell a child in order to feed the rest of their children.

Traditionally a prominent Pashtun farmer who owns his land is called a khan.[8] He will employ workers as well as members of his own family. Together the khan and his workers enjoy what is called a "patron-client" relationship. Each has obligations to the other which are understood. The client assists and obeys, not only in work but also in any situations where loyalty is called for. The patron protects, not only by offering wages or economic help, but also in other areas of life where a strong advocate is needed.

Farmland is inherited and is sold only as a last resort. Ideally all Pashtun men will own land. In reality, many do not and must work for others.

Regardless of the crop, land boundary disputes are common among farmers. "After all, just by plowing one extra furrow into your neighbor's land each year and moving the boundary marker a little, you can make a lot of their land your own in a decade."[9]

Water disputes are common also. Many rivers cycle annually from floods to trickles, so water availability is often an issue. Villages grow in relation to a network of irrigation channels. At regular intervals villagers will gather to clean the channels and repair any flood damage. Sometimes a group of musicians are hired to cheer them as they work.

When disputes arise, they may be tackled in several ways. A *jirga* is a grassroots community council among the Pashtun. Here the men of the area meet to discuss issues. Ideally the *jirga* is egalitarian and any man can speak up and push forward his opinions. This is where many local conflicts are raised, and sometimes resolved. Alternatively, a khan may serve directly as a mediator. If opponents will not yield, sometimes a mediator can elicit compromise by asking for it "in the name of God." Then "hard bargaining can be brought to a smooth end by a simple prayer that blesses and sanctifies the final agreement."[10]

These local conflict-resolution strategies show that although Afghans may have a warlike reputation, they also have traditional patterns for peacemaking. On a larger scale, when a battle has taken place, the losers can send an envoy

---

7   "A New Drug War," 28.

8   Azoy, "Reputation, Violence and *Buzkashi*," 99.

9   Barfield, *Afghanistan*, 34.

10 Barfield, 41.

to offer apologies. This is called *nanawati*. Similarly, when a *jirga* has settled a controversy between two tribes, the peace is called *rugheh*, and is sealed by laying a stone of peace, the *tizah*.[11]

In everyday interactions, Afghans demonstrate peace through hospitality. They take great pride in this. A simple village guest house may be located near the mosque. This usually contains a stove and several beds. When there are visitors, elders may drop in for a chat. In the morning a family head may arrive bearing breakfast, customarily a teapot full of hot milk and a loaf of bread. In their own homes, too, families delight in showing hospitality. There is even a proverb, "A house without a guest is like a house without God."[12]

Pashtunwali is the term used for a set of traditional values claimed by the Pashtun people. Other groups' values are similar. Besides hospitality, Pashtuns are said to value honor (they may or may not!), pride, family, loyalty, wisdom, bravery, strength, generosity, equality, the worship of Allah, and the unselfish love of a friend.[13]

How is equality demonstrated? Leaders are respected and followed, but no man wants to be subservient to another for very long. A laborer can switch to a new khan if he wishes. A military leader's command is temporary, calling forth loyalty during a given crisis. After the event, the leader will retain honor, but not necessarily power.

Even family relations are jousting competitions. It is true that families are units, as demonstrated by the fact that a family can be punished for the crime of one of its members, and insults against the family must be avenged. However, within the family itself there will be struggle. Cousin rivalry is so common that there is a term for it, *tiburwali*. Brothers often collide. Sons may try to dominate their fathers. Mothers-in-law rule their daughters-in-law. There is a proverb "The Pukhtun is never at peace except when he is at war."[14]

Surprisingly, there is one relationship that may be close and trusting. This is the tie with a true friend. Perhaps a person cannot be open with family members. They cannot be trusted deeply because they are rivals for resources. However, a man who is very fortunate may encounter a likeminded, empathetic outsider who can become a lasting confidante. Deep loyalty can develop between these friends.

All in all, in spite of the richness of friends and family, an Afghan farmer's life is difficult. "Subsistence agriculture in Afghanistan involves an almost-unimaginable daily life of toil, where one gets up at dawn because there is light and goes to sleep soon after dark because there is not. Such a physically-demanding

---

11 Wilber, *Afghanistan*, 116–17.

12 Monsutti, "Trust, Friendship and Transversal," 161.

13 Ahmed, *Social and Economic Change*, 47; and Spain, *Way of the Pathans*, 52.

14 Lindholm, *Generosity and Jealousy*, 31.

life makes people appear a lot older than they really are—that is, if they even survive long enough to look old."[15] In farmers' families, rural Afghanistan has some of the highest infant and maternal mortality rates in the world.

Because in old-style traditional Muslim society these conditions are seen as the will of God, this way of life is accepted. A farming family works to provide for their own needs. They do not struggle to increase their income. When they have enough, they ease up and take a little relaxation. Local artisans provide the tools and house furnishings that they require. They exist in a "world of reciprocal obligations." Although life is tough, "they can weather economic and political disruptions that would collapse more complex systems."[16]

Begin with the Land

Afghanistan lies at a crossroads of civilizations. It is a hard place, even with stunning lapis lazuli, mouth-watering pomegranates, and resilient residents. Much of the terrain is forbidding. Much of the land has been damaged by war, and the infrastructure smashed. Yet God is God not only of creation but also of new creations, new beginnings, new births. God resurrects and restores.

God takes delight in the landscapes, the geographical features, and the resource repertoires of his created world. His joy in these particularities shines through the words of Deuteronomy 8:7–9 when God recounts what he has given his people:

> A good land … with brooks, streams, and deep springs gushing out into the valleys and hills; a land with wheat and barley, vines and fig trees, pomegranates, olive oil and honey; a land where bread will not be scarce … a land where the rocks are iron, and you can dig copper out of the hills.

This is a lovely picture. Tragically, such beauty often is scanty, whether in Afghanistan or elsewhere. Land mines have been strewn through once-pristine fields. Cities have been hollowed out by war. Slimy slums suppurate. Fragrant white flowers have been crushed and transformed into heroin. Rivers roil with pollution, and their dirty water kills healthy toddlers. On the larger world scene, plastics proliferate: in the middle of the Pacific they spiral in a swirl as big as Texas. Again and again, we have desecrated God's world. Ugliness and despoilation trash the land and the sea. Our place is in deep trouble.

That is why creation is not the end but the beginning. After creation comes incarnation—God affirming the material world by inhabiting it. That is followed by sacrificial death, then resurrection, then restoration, and ultimately the magnificent, never-ending party to celebrate the cosmic King.

---

15 Barfield, *Afghanistan*, 38.
16 Barfield, 34.

Meanwhile, in history—in our time—Christ confronts the powers of destruction and infection and disinformation and pollution and all the other results of our sin. God in Christ makes restoration possible, both physical and spiritual. Nature is breathtakingly renewable. At the simplest level, we see new birth every spring, a season that Afghans love to celebrate in the *Nawruz* festival. More dramatically, after the sweeping desolation following volcanos and fires and, yes, wars, it is amazing to discover that forests do grow again and fish and animals return.

We can and we must help this process. Consider rivers. Many have become filthy. Some are toxic. Yet they can be cleaned up. In Oregon's Willamette River, for example, once-massive fish runs had dwindled until fewer than one hundred wild Chinook salmon were returning to spawn each year. That strain of salmon was going extinct. But Oregon's residents voted to clean up the river. In the 1960s a determined governor came into office. Strong action was taken—and the Chinook salmon came back to the Willamette.

Similar cleanups are happening in many places worldwide. Renewal and restoration are possible because of the regenerative power that God has programmed into this universe. Spiritually, too, new birth is possible, as Jesus told the seeker Nicodemus in John 3. Afghanistan needs renewal and restoration at every level.

What are the material realities facing a people? What are the resources, the skills, the trading networks? What problems do people face as they try to make a living, and how do they solve these? We have begun with these kinds of questions because the material world makes a difference—it channels the cultural patterns that flower into a way of life.

— CHAPTER 4 —

Women and Men

Afghan women are restricted today. This is condemned worldwide.
But what are normal roles for women in Afghan society?
The chapter includes:

- *A theology of culture as a context for affirming what is right and judging what is wrong*
- *Islam and women*
- *Global biases and women*
- *Afghan women in their homes and families*
- *Afghan women and money*
- *Dreams for Afghan women*

Nabila is in hiding. Two years ago she was a judge in Afghanistan's Supreme Court. It was part of her job to grant divorces to women whose husbands had assaulted or kidnapped them. Unfortunately, her work generated threats. If men lost their cases, they roared "I'll kill you!" when they exited from the court room.

After the national government changed in August 2021, hundreds of prisoners were released. Soon death warnings began to arrive for Nabila. She, her husband, and their three children swooped into hiding, like many of Afghanistan's two hundred female judges. It was simply too dangerous for them to keep working any longer. In some cases the government froze their bank accounts.[1]

"For the woman, either the house or the grave" is a traditional Afghan proverb.[2] There is a place for women, but it is limited. Basically, women belong at home. That inherited view has been resurrected by the

---

1 Zucchino, "Female Judges," A6.
2 Ahmed, *Mataloona*, xvii.

current Taliban government. Traditionally, while poorer women may find it necessary to go out into the public arena to work or shop, the ideal Afghan woman stays home most of the time.

Marriage, not education, is the goal for girls, according to the Taliban. Tragically, this sometimes means very young brides. In rare cases a girl as young as seven or eight years old is "sold" by her desperate, starving family to an older, wealthier groom who already has several wives. One young woman recently was exchanged for money to pay for her father's surgery. Another was married so that her family could pay to treat her brother's drug addiction.

Today twelve-year-old Samir laments her options. "My Auntie Teva had a textile store. She knew bookkeeping and handled government forms. My Auntie Latifa administered an office. As for me, I wanted to be a doctor or a teacher. But now girls' schools are closed."

Just getting to work or shopping for necessities can be stressful. Under the previous Taliban regime, women were not allowed to go out anywhere alone. A few cut their daughters' hair and dressed them as boys so as to have street-acceptable "male" chaperones beside them when they walked to their jobs. Clearly this was risky. Yet for the million widows living in the country, many with dependent children, a job was essential. Conditions are not quite as strict today, but many prohibitions and punishments threaten women, and the atmosphere remains scary.

Afghan Culture and Women

What is a woman? A cook, a housekeeper, and a mother for some man's children? A sex object? A lineal connection to important men? Or cheap labor? Or, negatively, is a woman a pollutant in society?

A woman is a person made in the image of God, potentially liberated by Jesus's death and resurrection, potentially empowered by the Holy Spirit, and commissioned for active service in God's world. Different cultures shape this differently. Some are more communal and others more individualistic. In communal societies, such as those in biblical times and in Afghanistan today, neither women nor men make many decisions by themselves. The family and community offer counsel and connections. When this goes well, it makes a person feel secure. It is comforting not to have to shoulder big responsibilities all by yourself.

Sometimes things do not go well, however. Through ignorance or selfish greed, a family may promote and even force an unwanted wedding to an undesirable mate. Or a community may prohibit a young person from pursuing their career choice. These life shocks happen to men, but even more often to women.

Has this always been so? Has Afghan culture generally restricted women? If so, isn't it a negative system that should be confronted and changed? Afghan people matter, certainly. But would it be any great loss if Afghan cultural patterns disappeared?

Yes. It would be a loss. Cultures are gifts of God. Even warped, misused, and in need of radical transformation, a cultural heritage is precious. Though it is experienced differently by people in different gender, income, or ethnic categories, though people change when globalization floods the world and they move from one land to another, still they need roots in order to feel whole and healthy. Even in a changing world we crave continuity.

Take the feast of *Nawruz*. In the springtime Afghan families gather to mark the beginning of the New Year. The snow has melted, the wheat and barley have been planted, and it is time to celebrate life. Special dishes are cooked. *Samanak* is a dessert made of wheat and sugar that requires two and a half days to prepare. *Haft-mewah* is composed of seven fruits, including walnuts, almonds, pistachios, red raisins, green raisins, dried apricots, and a fruit called *sanjet*.

During this holiday, picnics take place. Sports like *buzkashi* are played. This game involves teams on horseback who compete to lift and transport the carcass of a calf to a goal post a mile away, then bring it back, while warding off other players who want to snatch it away. It is raucous, dangerous, and highly competitive. Meanwhile, among the more peaceful activities at *Nawruz*, flowers are admired, especially red tulips. This festival is one of the cultural patterns that Afghans have developed over the centuries to celebrate God's good gifts. Even those who migrate to Europe or America will gather and feast if they can. This is a part of the heritage that they treasure.

Where did such cultural patterns come from? In the beginning, God created people in his image, endowing us all with a bit of creativity. Using this gift, humans have imagined and developed cultural patterns—cuisines, housing styles, family arrangements, agriculture techniques, economic exchanges, community groupings, governments, conflict-resolution strategies, games, music, and philosophies. As one poet said,

> When God made the world, he could have finished it. But he didn't. He left it as a raw material—to tease us, to tantalize us, to set us thinking, and experimenting, and risking, and adventuring. And therein we find our supreme interest in living.
>
> He gave us the challenge of raw materials, not the satisfaction of perfect, finished things.
>
> He left the music unsung, and the dramas unplayed.

He left the poetry undreamed, in order that men and women might not become bored, but engaged in stimulating, exciting, creative activities that keep them thinking, working, experimenting, and experiencing all the joys and satisfactions of achievement.[3]

Like the colors in a mosaic or kaleidoscope, contrasting cultures enrich God's world. This is a delight to God. The one who creates all kinds of hues and aromas and bird calls, and a boggling array of fish spangled across the oceans, and layers of diverse granites from grey to red to white to black under the soil, and billions of unique snowflakes and personalities—this is the God who makes different cultures possible. Diversity continues to the end of time, when the Bible describes people from every distinct tribe and language worshipping together around God's throne.

Afghan culture exists because God made Afghan people creative.

But what about the suffering that many Afghan women endure? Sadly, there is more to the story of cultures. We are not only created in God's image; we are also sinners. In every culture we have twisted God's good gifts. We have made idols of politics, sex, money, family pride, sports, art, fashion, and religion, and have used these to exploit and abuse others.

We are called, then, not only to appreciate our culture but also to confront it. Not only do we affirm God's good gifts within our culture. Simultaneously we must judge the patterns of idolatry and exploitation.

The New Testament describes "the powers" in two contrasting ways. On one hand, the powers that give order to our lives—government, education, media, religion, sports, art, family—are gifts of God: "For in [Jesus] all things were created: things in heaven and on earth, visible and invisible, whether thrones or powers or rulers or authorities; all things have been created through him and for him. He is before all things, and in him all things hold together" (Col 1:16–17).

Yet because we turn these good gifts into idols, we also must challenge them: "For our struggle is not against flesh and blood, but against the rulers, against the authorities, against the powers of this dark world and against the spiritual forces of evil in the heavenly realms" (Eph 6:12).

Jesus died to defeat the powers and rose to usher in a new kind of power in the greatest confrontation of all: "Having canceled the charge of our legal indebtedness, which stood against us and condemned us; he has taken it away, nailing it to the cross. And having disarmed the powers and authorities, he made a public spectacle of them, triumphing over them by the cross" (Col 2:14–15).

---

3 Stockdale, "God Left the Challenge," 20.

The "powers" in these verses refer both to spiritual entities and to cultural institutions that can become de facto idols.

Afghan cultures have infused order and joy and hope into their communities: Pushtun and Hazara, Turkmen and Nuristani, Uzbek and Baluch and Tajik and many others, each with their language, foods, family patterns, farming and herding traditions, celebrations and jokes. Tragically, as sinners Afghans also have developed exploitative patterns. So, for example, the sense of honor which is so admirable often deteriorates into an ugly and cruel drive for revenge. Such evil must be called out. It must be named and judged. But evil is not the bottom line. In the beginning and underneath it all are God's good gifts, the beneficial creativity to be treasured in Afghanistan as everywhere in the world.

This theology of culture will frame our understanding of Afghan women's lives. How are Afghan cultural patterns a blessing for women? How are they a curse? And how do different women experience these realities differently?

Islam and Women

Most Afghans are Muslims. Non-Muslims often believe that Islam restricts women and treats them poorly. Is that true? Are women oppressed in the Muslim world? Some are. But others would say, "Not at all!" Many Muslim women value the protection of the extended family and community. They enjoy women's gatherings and associations. It is true that men and women do not have equal rights, as we will see below. Certainly it is possible for women to be exploited in such a system. Family and community elders can exploit women and other less-powerful people to benefit the group. That is a danger. By contrast, in an individualist society, aloneness can be profoundly disempowering. When we think of women in Muslim societies, we would do well to remember that women in Bible times lived in cultures with limits much like traditional Muslim cultures today, and many of those biblical women thrived.

What are the differences between men and women under Muslim law? In inheritance, a daughter receives only half as much as a son. In a court of law, the testimonies of two women are required to balance the testimony of one man. In marriage, a man may have four wives at the same time. In divorce, a man has custody of the children after they pass a young age. Societies often ignore these laws, however. In Afghanistan, daughters generally do not inherit anything except their wedding dowry.

For his part, a Muslim man is not free to follow his own interests. He has a duty to support the family and protect them. A brother has some responsibilities toward his sister as long as she is alive. As for marriage, quite a few young men are married against their will because the family has arranged it.

In spite of the inequalities of Muslim law, many women would prefer to live under that system rather than in a secular democracy. Why? An extensive Gallup poll found that Muslim women worldwide strongly desire to live in a moral and God-fearing society. That is one of their highest values.[4] What do they consider a God-fearing society? At the most basic level, it is a community where prayer is practiced in the public square. Where God the Creator is mentioned in school science classes. Where chastity and modesty are taught in school health classes and practiced in interpersonal relations. Where the extended family matters, and grandparents and single aunts are not left lonely. Do they see this God-fearing, moral society in the secular West? No, they do not. So, even if they may not like the way Islam limits women, still they prefer to live under Muslim law.

In daily life, Afghan women do not spend a lot of time thinking about God. They are preoccupied with their duties, relationships, money, health, fashions, the changing seasons, social celebrations, and dangers and disasters. Women are not taught much about the *Quran*, the Muslim scripture, nor about doctrine. Instead, due to menstruation, pregnancy, or breastfeeding, they often find themselves in an "impure" state. Such impurity bars them from ritual prayers or fasting, though those are absolute requirements for Muslims. Lack of religious knowledge and frequent impurity add up to women's inherent "deficiency in religion," according to the prophet Muhammad.[5]

Still, women cry out to God. When they come to the end of their resources, they beg for supernatural help. Someone is sick. Or infertility blights a woman. In her distress, a woman will perform a magical ritual or visit the shrine of a saint. Yet she knows that this is second best. God is more than magic. God is the Creator who has endowed her with honor and dignity as his creature. Within her limited sphere, she is accountable to make choices that honor Him. But she does not know how.

Blaming Women

The Taliban government are not the only people with a dim view of women, and Afghanistan is hardly the only land where women have been demeaned. Men have been blaming women across time and space. Adam himself argued, "The woman you put here with me—she gave me some fruit from the tree, and I ate it" (Gen 3:12). That was Adam's excuse when God confronted him for his disobedience. The woman is to blame. The woman is responsible. The woman made me sin. Men in many cultures have echoed this.

---

4 Abdo and Mogahed, "What Muslim Women Want," A18.

5 Jafar, *Nahjul Balagha*, 177.

The honorable Christian theologian Tertullian thundered, "You (woman) are the devil's gateway, you are the unsealer of that (forbidden) tree; you are the first deserter of the divine law; you are she who persuaded God's image, man. On account of your desert, that is death—even the Son of God had to die."[6]

In India, when Christians began schools for girls in the 1800s, Hindus scoffed, "It is easier to teach our cows than our women." In the South Pacific, some tribes have rated pigs higher than women. Among Jews, a classic prayer recites, "I thank you [God] that I was not born a woman." Among Muslims, some have called women "tools of Satan." In secular society, "ditsy blondes" are stock stereotypes.

In Afghanistan when a boy is born, his father traditionally shoots a rifle 14 times. When a girl is born there are only 5–7 shots. In the better-class homes, women are secluded and largely invisible to outside society. However, Afghanistan has avoided some of the worst aberrations in the Muslim world. There is hardly any female genital mutilation here. Nor are women treated as "war booty" to be traded and sold, as occurred under ISIS in Iraq and Syria.

While men in many cultures have belittled women, this may change when a man has a daughter. Up to that point, he might have viewed women as useful tools, sources of pleasure, or lineal social connectors to other important men. But now, as his curious, bouncy little girl asks questions, he realizes she is a gifted human being whose potential should be not only protected but also nurtured and developed. Eventually some men begin to extend that understanding to all women.

Others are moved by the memory of their mothers, women like Ma Joad in John Steinbeck's *Grapes of Wrath*. For Ma Joad's poor migrant family, this faded woman,

> thick with childbearing and work ... [was] the citadel of the family, the strong place that could not be taken. And since old Tom and the children could not know hurt or fear unless she acknowledged hurt and fear, she had practiced denying them in herself. And since, when a joyful thing happened, they looked to see whether joy was on her, it was her habit to build up laughter out of inadequate materials. But better than joy was calm. Imperturbability could be depended upon ... [She was] a healer ... an arbiter ... She seemed to know that if she swayed the family shook, and if she ever really deeply wavered or despaired the family would fall, the family will to function would be gone.[7]

Many societies have women like that. Some simple soccer moms demonstrate this resilience. So do Afghan mothers who, like Ma Joad, face hard

---

6 Tertullian, "Apparel of Women," 164–65.

7 Steinbeck, *Grapes of Wrath*, 77.

times with grit and ingenuity and perseverance. Author Rashid Aalish's mother insisted that he learn English, regardless of where they were living. She had a dream for him, and determination. It paid off: his competent command of English led to graduate study and a PhD, as well as the ability to convince US government officials to let his family immigrate to America.

One of the tragedies of Afghanistan was that a generation of boys lost their fathers in the fierce fighting against the Russians in the 1980s. The Taliban gathered these boys up into male-only training camps. Separated from the normal interaction with women that they would have had in their families—with sisters, cousins, mothers, aunts, and grandmothers—these young men came to view women as strange, dangerous, polluting temptresses who must be controlled and confined.

House and Family

Cooking and childcare are round-the-clock preoccupations for Afghan women. In rural areas as well as many urban communities, water must be drawn from a well or carried from a water source. Cooking fires must be fueled, frequently with dung patties which the women shape into a size that is usable. Wheat and corn must be ground. Dough must be kneaded and bread baked. Chickens and other animals must be fed. Clothes and furnishings must be maintained and repaired.

Women help each other with this daily work since they live in extended family household compounds. Headed by an older couple, a compound will include several of the couple's adult sons and their families. The oldest woman, the matriarch, holds the keys to the larder and manages the coordination of the more complex tasks. Along with providing for the family's needs, women also produce goods for sale.

Hospitality is huge among the values that Afghans treasure, and this depends on women's work. Though they may never meet the guests for whom they cook, women take great pride in laying out a fine spread of dishes.

In many societies women enjoy shopping, but not in a well-established Afghan household. Men do the shopping. A woman leaves home for medical care, to visit relatives, or to visit a shrine. On these outings she wears an all-enveloping robe called a *burqa* to protect her from being viewed by strange men on the street. Covered by this robe she carries her private space with her into public life. However, poorer Afghan women are not so secluded. They work in the fields, weeding, clearing stones, harvesting, threshing, and cleaning seeds.

Marriage is the watershed moment that ushers a woman into the compound household where she will spend the rest of her life. A young man tells his mother he is interested in a certain woman, or his female relatives may look around for a suitable bride. In either case, his father and a group of related men will approach the woman's family and raise the possibility of a marriage. Cousin marriages are preferred, because all the parties are familiar with each other. The bride brings a dowry, and the groom's family pays a bride price, often of roughly equal value. Clearly marriage is more than an individual affair.

This system can work well, but sometimes is abused. Some marriages are arranged when children are very young. Quite a few young men, and certainly young women, feel pushed into marriage. Wives are more likely to be beaten when husbands feel coerced into marriage.[8]

But when a son is born, both husband and wife are overjoyed. This is a woman's highest honor. Afghan children play with dolls, marbles, balls, and kites. In poorer families, they transform sticks and mud into all sorts of imaginative creations. Boys use catapults to shoot stones at birds with great accuracy. In wealthier homes, children play with imported toys and digital devices. Children also do errands, running freely through streets to procure or deliver items for their house-bound mothers. At the end of the day, mothers may sing lullabies and fathers may tell stories. Tragically, infant mortality is high. Women in one region aim to have ten children to make sure that one will live long enough to support them when they are old.

Between husband and wife, warm personal communication is not expected. While a man knows a woman is necessary, he tends to spend little time with his wife. Instead, he goes out to socialize with a group of men, or welcomes them into his own guest parlor where women are not present except briefly to serve tea or coffee. Women find enjoyment with the other women in the household, although a young wife may suffer under her mother-in-law's bossiness.

A man does not consider his wife a friend. Actually she should fear him a little. Otherwise she might take risks with the family honor. Women are believed to be extremely passionate, and this distracts a man from his devotion to God. As the master, the husband may slap or hit his wife if he is so inclined. She may retaliate by nagging, screaming, performing magic against him, gossiping, or refusing to cook.

While Afghan women may not know the finer points of Islam, they do understand the concept of their people's honor and take fierce pride in it. Malalai was a nineteenth century heroine who waved her veil and chanted Pushtun poetry to spur men to battle against the British. Not surprisingly, the first girls' high school in Kabul, founded in 1921, is the Malalai Lycee.

---

8 Smith, "Between Choice and Force," 168.

Women value men who are dangerous fighters. According to a proverb, "Men are born to die. There should be mourning only when they leave behind no sons to raise their swords."[9] A man who runs away from a battlefield receives no burial ceremony, and his mother will be the first person to reject him. In a traditional song, a girl sings to her (hypothetical) lover:

> My sweetheart failed to show *tureh* (sword, bravery)
>
> I repent the romance I had with him last night!
>
> It is better to see bloodstains all over you
>
> Than to see you coming back home safe and sound as a coward.[10]

Afghan women's lives are not easy. Food and health care often are limited. Restrictions cause them problems, especially during violent political upheavals. Inequalities show up in particular ways. For example, rural women sometimes will ride on the roof of a bus while men sit on seats inside. In some places women pull plows while men guide them. Still, Afghan women take pride in the honor of their people.

Women's Money

A poor woman may bloom if she can open a business, no matter how small.

In cultures where it is normal for women to produce and control significant resources, they are empowered automatically. For example, if the local economy revolves around hunting and gathering food, the women who harvest greens, root vegetable, seeds, nuts, and berries are as crucial as the men who hunt animals. Every producer counts.

When grain agriculture develops, however, an economic system becomes more complex. Surpluses occur and classes emerge. Often a woman no longer needs to produce food. Now she is valued not for her productivity but rather for her beauty to be enjoyed by a man, or for her connections to her father or other important men. A woman's power declines relative to the men in her immediate group.

Grain agriculture has been present in Afghanistan for millennia. On top of strong local customs isolating women from men, this economic reality has limited women's access to their own money. While they may help grow or produce goods, rules of modesty keep them from being present at the point of sale. So they do not directly reap the profits. Yet many poor women desperately need money of their own, either because they are widows or because the men in the family do not have sufficient money or do not budget it well.

---

9 Wilber, *Afghanistan*, 94.
10 Wilber, 115.

There are exceptions to this cashless condition. On one of the rare occasions when a woman visits her parents, she may be given a goat. Then she can sell animal products like yogurt to other women, and pocket the income. Alternatively, she may acquire an animal by borrowing one from a neighbor, feeding and breeding it, and keeping the offspring.

Carpet-making is one way that Afghan women have made significant money. This is a renowned heritage craft. In the English language the word *afghan* refers to a knitted blanket, often draped over the back of a sofa or tucked around peoples' legs as they cozy up in front of a fireplace on a cold night. Among Afghan people, weaving a carpet on a loom—smaller for nomads and larger for settled people—is an honored art.

First, the weaver will set up the frame. Next she will hang balls of yarn from a horizontal arm. Then she will stretch up, grab a thread, twist it around the strings on the loom, tie it into a knot, cut the thread, and repeat. Every so often she will pick up a many-tined fork and pound the knots tightly together. In this way, gorgeous carpets come into being. Carpet-making is a job for young women because it is physically demanding and requires good eyesight. Sometimes men take the finished carpets to market, sell them, and keep the proceeds. At other times women may fulfill private orders or may market directly to women and receive the money themselves.

In recent years, more than a hundred NGOs have helped Afghan women start small businesses, although current government restrictions have whittled the number down. Some of these are "microenterprises" funded with "microloans." Given just a little money, a woman can raise a few animals, start a tiny food catering enterprise, or buy or borrow a sewing machine and become a tailor. As a rule, the loan agency will offer ongoing training on topics like product quality, inventory control, procurement of supplies, record-keeping, and marketing connections. If customers are men, a woman can employ a younger male relative to interface with them.

Rubia is an NGO-sponsored embroidery business that began in 2000 among Afghan refugees in Pakistan.[11] Later it moved into Afghanistan, into both rural and urban areas. "Mending Afghanistan stitch by stitch" is the motto. Rubia aims to be a grassroots effort, allowing women to work flexibly in their homes. They innovate from a base of traditional designs and dyes. For a long time there was no office, and group leaders and staff gathered in the Afghan director's home to make decisions. The membership expands along natural lines, particularly among paternal and maternal kin. In one region, the headmen of the ten largest clans were invited to select twenty women each to participate. This spread ownership of the program.

---

11 Lehr, "Mending Afghanistan."

When women have been hired as staff, several times their husbands have insisted on being hired too. These men have collected money from sales, kept records, escorted members who needed to be out and about, built and repaired equipment, promoted the program to other men, etc. Both women and men are paid directly for their work, and this is done in public to reduce gossip and rumors.

Quality products are essential so poor work is not accepted. To improve techniques, a scaffold of mentors has been developed, each training a group of women. Keeping work clean has been a problem. To address that, the program gives out soap and wrapping cloths, and rejects dirty work. This strategy has succeeded. While the US was the original market for Rabia's products, the program's reputation is so good that some embroidery has been commissioned to adorn garments in fashion shows in Paris and Milan.

"A $20 loan is really just a pretext to give a woman an opportunity to find out who she is, to open up her natural creativity." This saying has been attributed to Muhammad Yunus, the Bangladeshi economist credited with launching the microloan movement.[12] In Bangladesh, loans have inspired women to take responsibility for other areas of their lives, even to pursue the gospel.[13] At Rubia, the workers have taken the initiative to request literacy classes. These are held in homes, like all the other activities.

Resource management is a skill that many Afghan women share. It would be wrong to view them as though they have nothing. Rather, economic help should build on their strengths.

Dreams for Afghan Women

While traditional women stay home, this is not the case for all. Nabila the judge spent her days in the courtroom. Among the Afghan diaspora spread across the world are many articulate women who demonstrate leadership at local, national, and international levels.

Inside Afghanistan, educated women have tried to practice their professions and open the way for the girls of the next generation. When the Taliban were last in power and closed girls' schools, thousands of clandestine schools continued in homes. More ambitiously, Hazara women professors fled from the capital and set up a women's university in their own region, far from the center of government control. Classrooms were built from brick, mud, and straw. There was no electricity or running water. Yet families in the city sent

---

12 Yunus, "The MicroLoan," E1-3.

13 Missiologist Karen Scott has demonstrated the relationship between empowering women through microloans and their growth as Christian disciples in her dissertation, "The Influence of Community Development."

their girl children to study at this university. There were three hundred students and sixteen professors.

One professor explained why they did it. "We detest the ruling party. They are against all civilization. They are against Afghan culture. They are against women in particular. They have given Islam and the Afghan people a bad name. Their children are growing up with no education. They have only a knowledge of guns and opium. But we are building a new generation of Afghans who will lead the nation toward peace."[14]

Christians admire these women. Christians themselves often have set up schools. For example, in England during the early 1800s mass education was not prized. Neither girls nor boys in poor families could read or do math. It took a determined Christian named Hannah More to swim against the current and organize schools on Sundays for these poor children. Here they learned reading, math, and Bible. Employers objected: "Religion will be the ruin of agriculture ... It is thwarting the will of God to upend social order." However, by 1850, three-quarters of the "labor class" children between ages five and fifteen were enrolled in a Sunday school. This education was so crucial that Hannah More has been credited with "bridging Dickens' Two Nations," bringing together the rich and the poor through literacy and schooling.[15]

In 2022, the Afghan government once again closed girls' schools above the elementary level. Worldwide this has been condemned as a backward step not only for individual girls but for the nation as a whole. For Nabila the judge who is in hiding, what does the future hold? And for potential Nabilas of the next generation? Women are half of Afghanistan's population. The country cannot afford to neglect this resource.

But affirming women will not look the same in every culture. In Afghanistan the circle of community must be taken seriously. Sometimes, tragically, the community treats individuals badly, particularly women. A young adult may desire education, a career, a spouse, or a faith of which the family disapproves. Months of delicate negotiation may follow, involving trusted intermediaries, family members who advocate for the petitioner's point of view. Still, sometimes the young person—or older person—may feel constrained to break from their family's counsel so as to follow their own vision. In the end, people are not cogs in a machine or pawns in a system. Every person has thoughts and gifts and dreams. Opposing the community's advice is not ideal, but sometimes it happens.

Whenever possible, however, group relationships should be respected. Mary, the mother of Jesus, lived in a patriarchal society. She did not go to school. When we first read about her, she was an uneducated teenage woman

---

14 Rashid, "Sister Courage," 30.

15 Prior, *Fierce Convictions*, 161.

living under a brutal foreign colonial regime that employed crucifixions as punishment. Yet Mary had a strong positive sense of identity, both personal and communal. In her spontaneous prayer-song recorded in Luke 1, she comments knowledgeably about God's nature, her people's history, social justice and care for the poor, and God's personal blessing to her. Although she was unschooled, she was aware that she was part of a great story, and had thought about what that meant.

Like Mary, Afghan women who live in communal societies are not passive victims. In many spheres they are active decision-makers. They demonstrate competency and creativity. They are oriented holistically toward their families but also organize women's community groups. They earn money when they can. If they are educated, they practice professions. They do not lead mixed worship nor preach to men, but they may join women's religious gatherings.

Afghan women are social, economic, and spiritual actors. They want to live in a God-fearing society. From time to time they feel a need to tap into supernatural power. They would like to pray with some confidence that they are being heard. They wish they could understand the spiritual elements in their dreams. They would love to hear and recite beautiful Scripture, and to do so in community with other women. They want God to bless their children.

A few years ago in another Muslim country, I (Miriam) was invited to speak to a large group of women. I began with God's commission to Adam and Eve to serve as his *khalifa* (caliphs), to be stewards of the earth.

> *Assalamu Aleikum* (peace be upon you).
> It is an honor to talk with you about women.
> Why do we exist? Let us begin with Eve (Bibi Hauwa).
> Nabi Adam and Bibi Hauwa were created by God to be his *khalifas*—to take care of his earth.
> That is why we too were created. We do not exist for our own pleasure.
> We are created to worship God,
> To take care of our community,
> To be God's caretakers in our neighborhoods.

The women were delighted to remember that God honored them with responsibilities. In small groups they brainstormed excitedly about how to improve their own immediate environments. They wanted to use God's gifts to bless their society, to make his world better.

Like these women, Afghan women are persons created in the image of God, potentially liberated by Jesus's death and resurrection, potentially empowered by the Holy Spirit, and commissioned for active service in God's world.

— CHAPTER 5 —

Government Macro and Micro

How did Afghans' political contexts develop?
This chapter will examine:

- *Diverse communal identities contrasting with individualistic Western democracy*

- *Colonialism impeding growth in self-government*

- *Durrani Empire (1747 ff) modeling decentralized consensus governing*

- *British, Soviets, and Americans retarding Afghan government's maturing*

- *Taliban continues the rule of force*

Why did the Taliban take control of the government in Afghanistan? What led up to this? What was the role of the Americans? The Russians? The British? How have traditional Afghan political patterns contributed? What shape may future governments take?

The road towards forming a stable, all-inclusive, and pro-development government has been bumpy in Afghanistan. Despite experiencing different forms of government, Afghans consistently have failed to unite and cooperate with each other for the good of their society. For that reason, some scholars describe Afghanistan's experience of state formation as "try again, fail again, and fail better."[1] Except for the period between 1747–1880, when Afghanistan was a confederacy of regions and experienced relative peace and stability, the rest of Afghanistan's history is filled with constant political turbulence,

---

1 Easton, *A Systems Analysis of Political Life.*

ethnic conflict, civil war, and regime turnover. One after another, governments have failed to create sustainable stability, peace, and development.

Internally, during certain periods in Afghanistan's history the members of the royal family failed to agree on a set of governance institutions that would facilitate cooperation. During other periods, ethnic, religious, or linguistic political leaders failed to do so. Externally, major powers—such as Great Britain (1837–1919), Soviet Union (1950s–1989), the United States of America (2001–2021), and China, Russia, Pakistan, and Iran (since 2021) have dominated Afghanistan's domestic and foreign policies. The recent collapse of the Afghan government was yet another failure. Despite spending untold trillions of dollars, the government could not last even a week without the military and financial support of the United States and other members of the international community.

Why has there been so much failure and so little success? Why have Afghans not been able to unite and cooperate with each other to form a stable government? Is it because of the leaders? Or the governance institutions? What about the external powers?

Government in Poor but Developing Nations

In the past 250 years, five significant government systems have tried to rule Afghanistan:

- The Durrani Empire
- Abdul Rahman, dominated by the British
- Soviet Communists
- Afghan elite, dominated by international powers, especially Americans
- Taliban religious fundamentalist extremists

What factors have contributed to success or failure of each of these governments? Political scientists have different theories. Some scholars argue that successful governments must build on the patterns of local social groups, classes, tribes, and blocs. Other scholars argue that states develop in accord with broader processes, irrespective of local patterns.

Joel Migdal, in his prominent book *Strong Societies and Weak States*, takes the first position.[2] According to Migdal, successfully achieving and maintaining an orderly government depends on whether the state can satisfy the people's "strategies of survival." Trying to create a strong state while ignoring existing local social patterns will result in failure. Government is not autonomous. Especially in Majority World countries, local patterns must be taken seriously.

---

2 Migdal, *Strong Societies and Weak*.

By contrast, modernization theorists emphasize the coherence and homogeneity of society as a pre-condition for peaceful government. This will provide a framework for lively public discourse, the development of social trust, and ultimately democracy.[3]

But many nations in Africa, Asia, and Latin America are heterogeneous, with strong differences between tribes and ethnic groups. According to modernization theorists, such divisions based on patrimonial identity disrupt the possibility for democratic public discourse.[4] This view was strengthened during the 1960s, when newly independent states often failed to form stable governments. Instead, ethnic, religious, and linguistic leaders fought constantly over state power and resources and tried to outbid rivals rather than unite and cooperate. Many scholars concluded that democracy—or even peaceful co-existence—is next to impossible in heterogeneous societies.

Still, even when inter-group tensions persist, can some good government institutions be built? What "rules of the game" might smooth the way?[5] Modernization theorists have come to see that they must take existing informal institutions seriously. In the absence of functioning formal governance institutions, people throughout history have developed a variety of strongly rooted informal structures to regulate different aspects of life. Afghans, for example, have used informal structures to resolve disputes, to allocate water streams to different parts of their villages, and to appoint local leaders.

During Ahmad Shah's empire—the golden age of Afghan rule—the country was run by a set of khans and tribal leaders who collectively formed the government. Regions and provinces were controlled by Ahmad Shah's sons or by Durrani Sardars, a kind of local council. Judicially the state's role was limited. Disputes were resolved by appeal to religious *Sharia* law or to customary tribal codes, such as the code of *Pashtunwali* among the Pashtun clans. According to the first British envoy to the Durrani court, *Sharia* judges existed "in all considerable towns in the Caubul dominions, and they [had] deputies over the whole country … [but they] nowhere interpose unless an application is made to them."[6] While the state paid some of these judges, most were supported by the local inhabitants. Nor did the state impose any unified interpretation or systematic review of judges' decisions: *Sharia* judges had significant authority and autonomy on their own.

---

3 Lipset, "Some Social Requisites," 169.
4 Putnam, *Making Democracy Work*.
5 Reilly, *Democracy in Divided Societies*.
6 Elphinstone, "Account of the Kingdom," 263.

How to apply the law, whether customary or *Sharia*, varied among different groups and regions. For Pashtun clans who followed *Pashtunwali*, khans played an active role in the "adjustment of disputes between individuals."[7] However, among the Ghilzai clans "no Khaun of a tribe or Mullik of a village ever interfere[d] as a magistrate to settle a dispute, or at least a serious one," according to Mountstuart Elphinstone, the British envoy observing in the early 1840s.[8] Although disputes could be resolved through tribal councils consisting of neutral members or experienced arbitrators, disputants were free to choose whether or not to use them. In sum, while Ahmad Shah's Durrani Empire was strong in military expansion and conquest, it did not have strong national domestic institutions, as illustrated by the judiciary.

Informal mechanisms for resolving disputes have remained intact in Afghanistan despite numerous foreign interventions and efforts to change. Even during the US presence (2001–2021), more than 75 percent of Afghans resolved their disputes through informal mechanisms.[9] To Afghans, the informal justice system appeared to be more efficient, rapid, and corruption-free.

This has implications for creating successful rules and institutions at the national level: formal institutions need to complement or accommodate informal ones. If the new institutions compete or try to substitute for existing informal patterns, the formal institutions will not be sustainable. Nor will they achieve their ultimate goals, whether political stability or economic growth.

Colonial and Religious Distortions

Beyond heterogeneity, poor countries differ from modern Western democracies in another way. Western democracies developed their governments gradually, on their own time schedule and under their own power. These early democracies emerged in small scale settings with weak state bureaucracies. Localities engaged in decision-making through assembly and council. This facilitated the growth of consensus-oriented governance.

In those states, when rulers needed people for taxes and waging wars but did not control the economy, they had to leverage the consent of their people in order to govern. Such early democracies were present not only in Europe but also in pre-colonial Africa, the Middle East, and China, according to Stasavage.[10] Over time, however, states diverged as they developed. China and the Islamic Middle Eastern countries adopted strong top-down bureaucracies—autocratic

---

7 Elphinstone, 105.

8 Elphinstone, 151.

9 Asia Foundation, *Survey of the Afghan*.

10 Stasavage, *Decline and Rise*, 48.

structures. No longer did rulers need the consent of their people. By contrast, in the Western countries democracies continued to evolve, interweaving popular control with strong state governance over large territories.

Poor countries, unfortunately, have not been free to develop democracy on their own, gradually shaping consensus in increasingly larger groupings. Instead, external powers have intruded to dominate the decision-making process and determine the institutional path. Backed by financial and military resources, these powers have promoted certain local leaders and influenced and shaped regimes. They have done this directly and also indirectly by backing their own favored, loyal politicians. Across colonized areas in Africa, Asia, and Latin America, as well as in more recent liberal state-building efforts in countries like Afghanistan, Iraq, Somalia, and Haiti, local leaders have found it in their best interests to align with the institutional settings designed by external powers. Native leaders may hold the titles, but their influence is minimal.

This institutional shock is apparent in the relationship of past and present great powers vis-à-vis poor and developing nations. Afghanistan experienced this when Great Britain promoted indirect rule, when the Soviet Union spread a Communist regime, when the United States and Western Europe exported their own versions of liberal democracy, and today when China and Russia support an authoritarian government. All these external powers have one common characteristic: they disrupt(ed) the original, traditional form of governance. Tragically, once the institutional path is reshaped by foreign powers, subsequent leaders find it difficult to deviate. A trail of dependency stretches on ahead.

Religion also plays a role. The teaching of Islam, for instance, fits well with the hierarchical structure of governance common in Muslim nations. Islam does emphasize the importance of consultation and consensus, and commends specific qualities for leaders, such as piety, honesty, justice, and fairness. Still, this religion tends to endow leaders with excessive authority. In such circumstances, the society's peace, stability, and development depend solely on the leaders' performance as they exercise their power. The assumption is that the leaders are not corrupt or corruptible. Despite adopting Islamic constitutions, Muslim nations often fail to incorporate accountability mechanisms so as to hold leaders to account. In such societies, culture gets shaped by Islamic rules, as do informal and formal institutions.

Of course, some politicians in developing nations prefer top-down governance which is not answerable to the people. This is compatible with their own desire for power. Yet such structures significantly impede peace, stability, and development, and ultimately will fail.

Afghan Empire and Traditional Governance 1747–1880

The contemporary history of Afghanistan goes back to 1747 when the Durrani dynasty, led by Ahmad Shah, formed an empire. This kicked off the early democracy period, from 1747–1880. Within few years, Ahmad Shah expanded Afghan territory from Khurasan in the west to Kashmir and North India in the east, and from Amu Darya in the north to the Arabian Sea in the South.

Afghanistan at this time resembled a loose confederation of tribes more than a centralized state. Through indirect rule, the top leader exerted authority via a network of autonomous princes. He also maintained a role for tribal and customary authority.[11] Dupree characterized this period as "alternating fusion and fission" where "a charismatic leader arises in a tribal society and … unites several tribes into a confederation, which spreads as far as its accumulated power permits, creating an empire, not a nation-state."[12]

During this period, localities relied on informal, traditional mechanisms to run their affairs, as described earlier. They supported Ahmad Shah's wars of conquest by providing taxes and soldiers.[13] Local leaders collected taxes, sent a certain amount to the central government, and kept the rest for their own affairs. However, many provinces yielded no revenue at all to the central government, according to one account.[14] The state bureaucracy apparently was absent in some areas and weak in others. Localities exercised a lot of autonomy.

First Shock: The British

After Ahmad Shah died in 1773, the consensual, traditional form of governance lasted only until 1880. His grandson started a power struggle which significantly undermined the relationship between the king and the regions. New taxes, new Sardars, and conflict among the Durrani brothers weakened the political order. Meanwhile, Great Britain was eyeing Afghanistan. This would usher in what has been called the Great Game, leading to major changes in Afghanistan's governance.

The Great Game was a political and military confrontation between the British and Russian empires. It lasted for most of the nineteenth century, focusing on Afghanistan and neighboring territories. At that time both the British and Russian empires were spreading out. Britain recently had conquered India, and Russia was progressively absorbing Tashkent, Bukhara, Samarkand and other points to the south. Britain wanted to protect its Indian occupation from possible Russian expansion, and also its key sea trade routes. In particular,

---

11 Hechter, *Containing Nationalism*.

12 Dupree, *Afghanistan*, xix.

13 Dupree, xix.

14 Barfield, *Afghanistan*.

Britain wanted to stop Russia from gaining a port on the Persian Gulf or the Indian Ocean. Afghanistan would serve as a buffer zone, Britain decided.

So Britain initiated two Anglo-Afghan wars (1839–42 and 1878–80) and finally installed their own puppet king in Afghanistan. "Transformation of Afghanistan from a group of trivial and warring principalities into one state ruled by a dependent of the government of India" was Britain's strategy.[15] Besides defending against Russia's threat, developing Afghanistan into a so-called modern state would foster Britain's political and military goals in the region.

Because Britain favored indirect rule, it installed Abdul Rahman as the new king of Afghanistan and supported him financially and militarily. Known as the "Iron Fist," Abdul Rahman took it upon himself to transform the existing consensual, traditional form of governance. He stamped out the middlemen—tribal and customary leaders, as well as religious authorities—whom he viewed sources of political disorder. To modernize government, he centralized the state apparatus, something that had not even existed in Afghanistan before. He emphasized two goals: first, concentrating all state affairs, even trivial things, into his own hands; and second, creating a strong army to impose his power throughout the country.

Abdul Rahman divided Afghanistan into six provinces—each headed by a governor loyal to him. These provinces were Herat, Kandahar, Kabul, Farah, Badakshan, and Turkestan. Unlike his predecessors, he imposed strict control over the provinces. Subdivisions were governed by officials who were appointed on the basis of personal loyalties, ethnic and tribal solidarities, *Sharia*, and customary laws.

Abdul Rahman formalized and bureaucratized all aspects of administration so as to define the clear scope of responsibilities for officials at higher and lower levels. He reorganized the civil and judicial administrations and adopted specific laws to bring these sectors under his direct control. Simultaneously, with Britain's support, he rather brutally suppressed any internal opposition against his excessive centralization policies. "Wholesale executions and deportations usually followed ... the conquest of independent areas."[16]

During this period, Afghanistan's national boundaries were drawn, including a twelve-hundred-mile Russo-Afghan border on the north and the infamous sixteen hundred mile Durand Line on the east. That Line split the Pashtu-speaking people in two. It became a lightning rod for violence during all the decades that followed. Russia later mocked the Durand Line as one of the failures of the British occupation.

Ironically Abdul Rahman himself recognized that he was stuck in an untenable situation when he mused, "How can a small power like Afghanistan,

---

15 Ingram, "Great Britain's Great Game," 160–71.

16 Dupree, *Afghanistan*, 416.

which is like a goat between these lions, or a grain of wheat between two strong millstones of the grinding mill, stand in the midway of the stones without being ground to dust?"[17]

Soviet Centralization

Thanks to Abdul Rahman's centralization, Britain was able to dominate Afghanistan's domestic and foreign policy for almost half a century. Under successive kings the centralized governance system continued, moderated by less aggressive policies vis-à-vis ethnic, religious, and linguistic minorities and opposition groups.

World War I and the turn of century changed the great powers' calculations and areas of interests. In 1919 Afghanistan claimed its independence from Britain during the third Anglo-Afghan war. Russia had been providing subsidies to the Afghan king for some time, but had to withdraw from Afghanistan during the tumultuous decades surrounding the two world wars.

After World War II ended, the Cold War began. Then the Soviet Union returned to Afghanistan, motivated by competition with the United States. This time the Soviet Union stayed for almost half a century, from the1950s to1992. Continuing the centralized government model, they transformed Afghanistan into a communist society over three decades. Educational, social, and cultural programs eventually gave rise to the first political parties in Afghanistan. These formed a communist regime for a decade. The Soviet Union also changed the shape of public administration by adding Soviet features such as a top-down bureaucracy to areas like general government structure, rules of decision-making, and employment.

Economically, the Soviet Union initiated the first five-year development plan in Afghanistan, following the model of Soviet central planning. In terms of trade, the Soviet Union became Afghanistan's main international business partner: more than 90 percent of Afghanistan's trade was conducted with the Soviet Union. Socially and culturally, Soviet advisors controlled all Afghan ministries, including education, culture, and information. Soviet advisors significantly changed the curriculum and teaching materials of schools and universities and oversaw the content of the press and media. Back home, the Soviet Union accepted tens of thousands of Afghans as students in Soviet universities.

Given the secular nature of the Afghan government at that time, the religious community was targeted. Many religious leaders disappeared. Some were killed. Meanwhile, the Afghan government started to redistribute lands and wealth and to restructure public administration, appointing new administrators who were absolutely loyal to the government.

---

17 Dupree, 417.

All in all, the Soviet Union continued the strategies of Great Britain: centralization and external domination. Adding Soviet features further concentrated the government and distanced Afghans from their traditional, consensual governance style.

US Liberal Democracy Continues Centralization

The Sovietization of Afghanistan only served the interests of the Soviet Union. It did not help Afghanistan create a stable, all-inclusive, pro-development state. Tragically, when the Soviets withdrew in 1992, Afghans could not agree upon a government. Civil war broke out between 1992 and 2001. During that window, the Taliban emerged.

Simultaneously, however, a new chapter in Afghan history opened in 2001. On September 11, terrorists attacked vital sites in the United States. Some of those terrorists had Afghan roots. The 9/11 attacks drew the US into Afghanistan, primarily for counterterrorism purposes, but ultimately for a state-building mission.

With the US came new hope for democracy and development. Some $150 billion for non-military sectors flowed into Afghanistan from 2001 to 2020, plus billions more from other allies and international organizations. This money funded education, health care, governance reforms and infrastructure, including schools, hospitals, roads, and other major construction projects. International aid helped construct and pave thousands of miles of roads and streets. Other infrastructure projects included hydroelectric dams and solar power plants to generate electricity, bridges, irrigation, and clean drinking water projects.

In education, far more students enrolled in school. The number of students jumped from 900,000 in 2001 to more than 9.5 million in 2020. Foreign aid helped build about twenty thousand elementary schools, and universities multiplied sharply. Afghans enrolled in higher education programs soared from seven thousand in 2001 to about two hundred thousand in 2019. There were no female college students in 2001, but there were 54,861 in 2019. The percentage of female students reached 39 percent in 2020, versus an estimated five thousand girls altogether in 2001.[18]

Likewise, access to health care expanded for most of the population. During this twenty-year period, life expectancy increased by about a decade, to 64.8 years in 2019, according to the World Bank.[19]

Afghanistan also made progress in governance reform, adopting a new constitution in 2004 that established a framework for liberal democratic

---

18 USAID, "Afghanistan."
19 WHO, "Afghanistan Health Systems."

governance and protected human rights. The nation held four presidential and provincial council elections and three parliamentary elections. Hundreds of new laws and regulations were adopted regarding education, health, insurance, budgeting, mining, women rights, and land titling.

As the third modern great power in Afghanistan, the United States had its own brand of state building when dealing with a developing nation: liberal democracy. However, although this could have facilitated consensual governance, the US and Afghan elites chose to continue the old, failed, centralized governance system. They did add some minor democratic features, such as elections, weak checks and balances, and separation of powers. The nation readopted the 1964 constitution, while changing from a constitutional monarchy to an Islamic Republic with a unitary presidential system. Yet Afghanistan continued the centralized governance system that Great Britain had imposed in the nineteenth century and that was later Sovietized. The United States, like those earlier powers, favored centralization over the decentralization which might have strengthened self-rule.

This turned out to be disastrous. In the post-2001 system, all political, fiscal, and administrative authority was concentrated into the hands of the president. Politically, the president could appoint almost all officials at all levels, including ministers, Supreme Court Justices, governors, and district governors. Fiscally, the president had a hold on planning, budgeting (formulation, allocation, and execution), and taxation. Administratively, the central government dominated all procurement and administrative affairs. The post-2001 governance system was in no way aligned with the traditional Afghan culture of governance. Natural state formation and democratization were disrupted once again. This ultimately resulted in the waste of trillions of dollars, the death of hundreds of thousands of Afghans and foreigners, and worst of all, the collapse of the Afghan government and the Taliban takeover in 2021.

The Taliban

So far, the Taliban's performance—their interim cabinet and their other domestic, exclusive policies—do not suggest that they have learned from history. More importantly, their financial dependence on countries like Pakistan, China, and Russia suggests that once again external powers will determine Afghanistan's political future.

The Afghan people themselves still long for honest, wise, culturally appropriate, self-sacrificing leaders who can work together in a true community across this diverse land. For those who want something better, Jesus the Servant-Leader may be worth studying.

Chapter 6

What the Taliban Want

Six types of Islam are practiced in Afghanistan:
Sunni Islam, Shia Islam, Ismaili Islam, Sufi Islam,
Reformist Islam, including Taliban and ISKP, and Folk Islam.
How can these various Muslims make sense of the gospel?
Four bridges are suggested.

The earth shakes. Smoke billows and obscures whatever may be nearby. Sound roars. A ceiling beam crashes down. Walls crumble, section by section. Shrieks rip through the air—"Help! Oh, my leg! My chest! My head! Where are you, son? Oh Allah!"

Just a minute before, voices had murmured, garments had rustled, and bodies had shuffled, rising and lowering as worshippers prayed. Someone had sniffled. A cart had rattled by outside.

Now a bomb has exploded in this mosque. Through the cavernous space under the soaring mosaics, people groan and wail. Toxic fumes make them cough and choke as they stumble and crawl, trying to find a way out. Fire arcs across the floor. Mangled legs, arms, and even heads protrude under the haze.

Who would invade this sacred space to murder innocent worshippers? Probably ISKP, a Muslim fundamentalist group that is struggling for power in Afghanistan. The country itself is governed by the Taliban, another fundamentalist group that grabbed the reins in 2021.

What do these fundamentalists want? What are they reacting against? What do they hope to build? Do they represent authentic Islam? Overall, what is Islam in Afghanistan today?

What Muslims Believe

God is the foundation of everything in the universe, according to Muslims. This God is not a vague force or an abstract grand principle, but a person who communicates with human beings. God created us, God regularly sends prophets and Scriptures to show us how we ought to live, and God expects us to respond with thanks and obedience. Allah is the name that Muslims use for God.

Although Muhammad (d. 532) was the prophet who made these teachings explicit, Muslims believe that there were earlier prophets, including Adam, Abraham, Moses, David, and Jesus. Most of these holy men received Scriptures from God, so Jews and Christians who share these prophets are known as "people of the book," meaning people who have received some of God's revelation. The final and most authoritative Scripture, the *Quran*, came to Muhammad.

Around the world Muslim men gather in mosques, especially on Fridays, to pray together and hear a sermon. Women may attend, keeping toward the back. More often women will pray at home or in women's worship and study groups. Regular Muslim rituals include circumcising boys, reciting a simple creed (*shahada*), reciting prescribed prayers five times daily (*salat*), giving a sort of annual tithe (*zakat*), and participating in the annual month of fasting (*Ramadan*) and once-in-a-lifetime pilgrimage to Mecca in Saudi Arabia if possible (*hajj*). The joy of a life of faith is displayed in several annual religious feasts. All of this is experienced within the community of believers (*ummah*), which is valued highly by Muslims.

Christians and Muslims have a great deal in common. For Muslims, Jesus is one of the greatest prophets. They believe he was born of a virgin, taught authoritatively, performed miracles, and will be a key figure in the final judgment. In the *Quran*, Jesus is called the Word of God, the Spirit of God, and even Messiah.

Yet the ways we understand Jesus constitute the key difference between Muslims and Christians. Muslims cannot believe that God would lower himself to take on human form, much less undergo death, the ultimate experience of human vulnerability. Jesus did not die on the cross, nor rise from the dead, in Muslim understanding. But this is the crux of the Christian faith. This is the demonstration of God's essential nature. This is the forgiving, liberating, transforming center event of history. Muslims set aside Jesus's divinity, his death, and his resurrection. So, although the two "Abrahamic faiths" are close, a deep abyss plunges between them. That dividing reality is the Lord Jesus Christ.

For Muslims, human beings do not need a Savior. We are not sinners: we are just ignorant. We need training in righteousness, and that is what the regular rituals of Islam provide.

Key Muslim Leaders

When Rashid was a child in Afghanistan, he encountered three types of Islam as his family moved from one location to another. Each type deferred to a different leader. This was confusing to him. When he worshipped in one locale, he had to approach God through one leader, but when he worshipped in another place he had to honor a different man in order to be pleasing to God. "Why can't I reach out to God directly?" he wondered. That was his heart cry when he heard about Jesus Christ. What a relief it was to discover that he could go to God directly, with no human leader in between.

Sunni Islam

What were the three types of Islam that Rashid encountered? First, Sunni Islam. Around AD 600 the Prophet Muhammad began teaching about God. There had been earlier holy men, like Abraham. They were considered Muslim, since "Islam" means "submitted to God." However, God's full and final revelation came through Muhammad. He himself was not a formal religious leader but a merchant trader. Occasionally he would retire into a cave to meditate on spiritual things. During his meditations, an angel began to appear to him, he testified. After his death, records of his recitations of the angel's words were gathered. These formed the text of the *Quran*. A much shorter book than the Bible, it includes praise to God, some stories similar to those in Genesis and in the Gospels, and advice for military campaigns, general social living, and worship practices.

One God—that was the Prophet Muhammad's core emphasis. During his lifetime, most people believed in spirits. Some Christians bowed before saints, and some Jews and Christians used magic. Muhammad said, "No. There is only one God. The foundation of the universe is one God. This is not a vague force, but a person with characteristics of truth and justice who wants to communicate with human beings." Of course, this belief in God's unity was shared by Jews and Christians. Still, in practice it often had been ignored.

Scriptures were sent by God over the centuries, Muhammad taught, including the Torah to Moses, the Psalms (*Zagreb*) to David, and the Gospel (*Injeel*) at the time of Jesus. The final and most important Scripture was the *Quran*, which was sent to the Prophet Muhammad. Besides these seminal sacred revelations are books known as *Hadith*. These are composed of wise sayings and interpretations, including many attributed to Muhammad. Gathered over succeeding centuries into several collections, *Hadith* are known by the names of their editors, and collators, such as Bukhari. As well, there is Muslim law (*Sharia*). Within the general framework of *Sharia*, Sunnis have four major schools of law. Shiites also have several legal traditions.

For Muslims, Scripture should be received and recited more than it should be analyzed. Believers ought not to intellectualize too much. More than speculating about Scripture, they should respect and obey it. Consensus (*ijma*), reason (*ijtihad*), and analogy (*qiyas*) figure in Scripture discussions, but as a general rule traditional interpretations are honored.[1]

Prayer, like Scripture, is foundational. When the mosque loudspeaker summons people, believers are to pause what they have been doing, wash, and line up with others in order to bow and kneel and raise hands together. They do this five times a day, reciting a standard prayer. At other times—before eating, writing, teaching, or having marital sexual relations—a Muslim is encouraged to whisper a very brief prayer, to remember that this act is part of God's gifts. The day is punctuated with remembrances of God through regular prayer.

Shia Islam

Almost from the beginning, unfortunately, there was fighting among the believers. Fighting was not unusual, because these people came from a warring background. However, some of the conflict was internal: Muslims took up arms against each other. In 680, fifty years after Mohammad's death, his grandsons Hassan and Husain were killed. For some grieving believers that was the breaking point. "We have erred," they said. "We have been following the wrong leaders. We have been listening to appointed caliphs when we should have been following the Prophet's own family." They transferred their allegiance to the line of Ali, Mohammad's son-in-law. This sector became known as Shia Islam.

Today Shia Islam is centered in Iran, next door to Afghanistan. Both Sunnis and Shiites honor the Prophet Mohammad, the *Quran*, and basic precepts like the creed, prayer, pilgrimage, and fasting. There are a few ritual differences. Shiite religious leaders like Ayatollahs tend to lead more dominantly. The prophets Ali and Husain are given special honor. Most distinctive to Shiism is an annual commemoration of the death of Husain. He is viewed as a martyr who gave his life for the people. Known as *Muharram*, the commemoration lasts ten days. It is marked by public reading of the story of Husain's death, and by parades. In these, people who have taken vows during the year may beat or flagellate themselves. Similar to Passion Week in former times in some Christian countries, there may be mourning and weeping when the heroic figure's death is recounted.

Ismaili Islam

The third type of Islam that Rashid encountered as a child was Ismaili Islam. Ismailis grew out of the Shiite branch. They split because of a difference over the succession of leaders. In the past century the head men among the Ismailis have been the Agha Khans. Ismailis are known for cooperative investments and

---

1 Denny, *Introduction to Islam*, 163–71.

sound financial management, with business connections in many countries. They also sometimes have welfare programs for their own people, including health care, education, and insurance. In Afghanistan many of the Hazara people in the north are Ismaili.

"Which is the important religious leader?" Rashid wondered. "The Prophet Muhammad? The Prophet Husain? The Agha Khan?" At times he was directed to one, and at other times to another. "Which one could lead me to God?" he questioned.

Religion of the Heart

That kind of question has stirred Muslims for a long time. In the earliest years, Islam was a religion of the open desert spaces. As the movement spread among Arabs around the Fertile Crescent and along the southern Mediterranean, as well as to Persians and others, it became apparent that the middle of the desert was not a convenient base for a multinational faith. Damascus, with all its land and sea connections, became the new center.

But Damascus' sophistication, wealth, and power bothered some sincere believers. So did the increasing religious bureaucracy. By 700, the theological wrangling of the clerics and the luxuries of the caliphs had disillusioned some Muslims. "How can we encounter God authentically?" they wondered. "We need to sweep away all these false layers and get down to the true religion, the bedrock. We need to go back to the simple worship of God."

Sufi Islam

Out of this sincere longing, the Sufi tradition was born. Sufis were mystical Muslims. Through a series of spiritual disciplines, they hoped to experience God's presence. Sometimes they chanted all together. Sometimes they moved through whirling dances. As these activities drew them into trances, Sufis experienced release and exaltation. Some felt that they were absorbed into God. On a day-to-day basis, Sufis were mentored in brotherhoods.

Today there are still about 75 Sufi orders existing worldwide. Some of these are more than one thousand years old. It is not necessary to leave Sunni Islam to join a Sufi order. Rather like charismatic Christianity, Sufism is a set of spiritual practices that can be experienced in varying degrees on top of an orthodox foundation. An order that is well established in Afghanistan is the Naqshbandi.

Al-Ghazali (d. 1111) was one of the greatest Muslims of all time. He was a towering theological intellect and the author of comprehensive tomes. Yet he felt the need for a more personal relationship with God. Ultimately he became a Sufi. Another famous Sufi was a woman named Rabia. She spoke movingly about the hunger of the heart: "Oh God, if I worship you from fear of hell, burn me there.

If I worship you from hope of heaven, exclude me from that. But if I worship you from love of your own self, then withhold not from me your eternal beauty."[2]

There is much that is admirable in Sufism. However, it shares a danger that is common in mysticism: it can slide into doctrinal looseness. In Muslim history, "sober Sufis" came to be distinguished from "intoxicated Sufis." While the former worshipped in ways that were consistent with standard beliefs, "intoxicated Sufis" were unpredictable. In their transcendent moments they could erupt with all sorts of heresy. Some were executed for blasphemy, like Al-Hallaj (d. 922).

It was Islam's very success that opened the door to heresy. As the faith spread beyond the Arab world, it came into contact with other religious traditions like Greek and Hindu. Here Sufis encountered exciting new mystical ideas, such as Hindu teachings about God being present in all of creation. Over time some Sufis began to look for God inside themselves. They aimed to ascend through stages of spiritual disciplines until they could become "perfect men."

Eventually even the prophet Muhammad came to be reimagined as a universal spiritual being, as the cosmic center who has existed from eternity. No longer was he simply God's messenger. Now viewed as the eternal mediator for all mankind, Muhammad began to function almost as a deity. Understood as the ideal intercessor with Allah, Muhammad became the focus of prayers. Although this was not the way Muhammad had understood himself, this belief became hugely popular.

Going further, Sufis believed that Muhammad channeled power, blessing, and influence to local spiritual leaders, who are revered as saints after their deaths. In Afghanistan, "almost any stone thrown will hit the shrine of a saint."[3] Some shrines are reputed to cure insanity, others to cure infertility, and one reportedly can cure the bites of rabid dogs. At one shrine, women who want to get pregnant may pick up dirt and eat it, possibly connecting with Mother Earth. Some shrine caretakers sell copies of verses from the Quran which can be used as magical charms. Overall, such grassroots spiritual leaders endowed with supernatural power help people solve problems, achieve their hopes, and get protection from evil forces.

A Purifying Reformation

Fundamentalist Reform Islam

"Enough! Pollution of the true faith must stop!" This is the cry of religious reformers. Take, for example, an Arabian named Mohammad bin Abdul Wahab

---

2 Cragg, *House of Islam*, 68.

3 Dupree, *Afghanistan*, 105.

(d. 1797). After studying in Damascus and Persia, and observing the deplorable syncretism in those places, Wahab returned to Arabia determined to purify the faith. Fortuitously he caught the attention of Muhammad ibn Saud, whose family continues to rule Saudi Arabia today. Wahabism became the official branch of Islam in that country.

Muslims must return to the basic teachings of the *Quran* and the *Hadith*: this is what Wahab thundered. True knowledge rests in the oneness of God. That is the fundamental reality. There are no mediators, neither cosmic nor local. Muslims must not pray to Muhammad or ask favor from saints. Nor can they build shrines or visit saints' graves with candles and offerings. Even grave custodians are forbidden. Muslims must not make pilgrimages except to three approved destinations, Mecca, Medina, and Al Aqsa. They must not celebrate on Muhammad's birthday or call down any blessing on him. Wahab also condemned the practices of Sufi orders.

All that we need to know to live together in society is contained in the *Quran* and *Hadith*, Wahab argued. All social issues are addressed explicitly in these books. Any other authorities or ideologies are to be rejected, even movements like humanism. Over time similar reformers arose in Pakistan, Iran, Syria, Indonesia, and other countries.

Many came to believe that "godless" Western influences had corrupted "godly" Muslim societies. During the nineteenth and twentieth centuries, European powers rolled across the Muslim world. France took Syria and parts of North Africa; Britain took Palestine, Egypt, and India; Italy took Libya. The Netherlands tightened its hold of three centuries on Indonesia.

In Afghanistan invasions were nothing new: Persians, Mongols, Uzbeks, and Indians had been pushing in for millennia. What was new in the twentieth and twenty-first centuries were the devastating weapons. Afghanistan was scratched when Britain stretched out from India, but it was never dominated for long. Yet today the land lies scarred from the wrangling between Russia, the US, and Afghans.

Overall, foreign control has been harder for Muslims to tolerate than it would have been for Christians if the situation had been reversed. Christian theology offers a framework for understanding suffering in a sinful world. Muslim theology does not offer such a framework. Muhammad did not die on a cross. Instead, he went from victory to victory. Godly Muslims should experience this too, they believe. So alien colonial rule made no sense. How could this be God's will?

Furthermore, Muslims ideally do not believe in "separation of church and state." A moral government must be based on God's law. Yet colonial powers replaced Muslim law with secular codes. This splintered the unity of godly communities, in their view. Since independence, much of the violence in

Muslim countries has been between Muslims who want to restore theocracies versus Muslims who believe that desacralized law codes work better.

All this arouses fundamentalists. Foreign ungodliness pollutes the Muslim world. There must be cleansing. This is their strong belief. In the view of Afghan thinker Gulbuddin Hikmatyar, although the Soviets withdrew, the secular West was no better: "Their materialistic economy has no future, their moral fiber is torn by divorce and abortion, and their health is threatened by the specters of drugs and the epidemic of AIDS."[4]

Mosque bombings in Afghanistan explode out of convictions like these. A passion to purify the faith propels them. Unquestionably, this passion is perverted. The method is intolerable. Yet the goal is understandable. Clear out the idolatry, the hedonism, and the ungodliness, and cut to the clear, beautiful worship of God. This is the religious reformer's dream.

ISKP versus Taliban

Nothing in Afghanistan is uncomplicated, so there is not just one fundamentalist Islamic movement, but two: the Taliban, who are in power, and the Islamic State Khorasan Province (ISKP). It is the ISKP who have been bombing mosques and schools and power stations.

Like Catholics and Protestants who sporadically burned and savaged each other during the 1600s, these rival Afghan movements share much common doctrine. However, they are divided by social and political rivalries, and by old grievances that fester. As for their doctrinal differences, ISKP aims for a global caliphate. The movement is connected to ISIS in Syria and Iraq, and indirectly to the disaster of September 11, 2001. In its struggle, ISKP targets not only Christian-heritage nations but also Muslim-heritage governments or individuals who appear to be apostate. *Takfir*, excommunicating and executing heretics, is a key principle. This powers their fight with the Taliban.

Scarcely any other countries recognize the Taliban as a legitimate government because of the way it usurped power in August 2021 and because it has a history of repression. When it was last in power, from 1996 to 2001, it limited women severely, closed some schools, and targeted religious and ethnic minorities with violence. There were some large massacres. Much priceless art in the National Museum and National Library was destroyed in the cause of winnowing out ungodly influences. The massive, ancient, and strikingly unique Buddha statues in Bamiyan Valley were dynamited and sledgehammered to bits. The Taliban government also killed dozens of health care workers, both foreign and Afghan, in opposition to polio vaccinations. The Taliban feared these shots would make children sterile. Later, to their credit, they reversed their position.

---

4 Barfield, *Afghanistan*, 231.

Beyond opposing eating pork and drinking alcohol—common Muslim taboos—the Taliban also at times have banned gambling, TV, internet, photos, football, chess, and kite and pigeon flying. At one point the government even killed pet pigeons. Believing that pictures lead to idolatry, officials have painted over road signs that indicate livestock crossings. On the positive side, the Taliban would like to be credited for bringing a significant amount of order and unity to an "ungovernable land,"—a goal that has eluded multiple other powers—and for holding the line against both atheistic communism and Western decadence.

What do the Taliban want? At their best they want a simple, clean worship of God in word and deed. In actuality they are far from achieving this, due to ignorance, human self-centered depravity, and the tendency of power to accelerate corruption if not reined in by countervailing checks and balances. Still, they have glimpsed an ideal. They would resonate with the psalmist who said, "The fear of the Lord is the beginning of wisdom" (Psalm 111:10). Muslim fundamentalists would echo that psalm. God is foundational. All wisdom rests with him. Anything that distracts from that is insignificant. Let us focus on the priorities that matter.

What about My Toothache?

But does Allah care about me? That is the heart cry of ordinary people in Afghanistan, as in countries around the world. Yes, Allah may care about the universe. He may care about society. What about my toothache? My bankruptcy? My divorce? Those are the concerns that overwhelm me. Where can I find help beyond my family and my community? If supernatural resources exist, can I tap into them?

Folk Islam

People sense that there is more to life than material and social patterns. There is a spiritual dimension, and it is probably important. If God appears to be distant and unapproachable, there may be supernatural forces closer to hand, namely spirits. Magical rituals enable people to access help from benevolent spirits and protect their family against malevolent ones. Such rituals are pervasive in Afghanistan, where people do not read or understand Arabic, the language of their Scriptures, and generally receive minimal teaching on Islam. "The Islam practiced in Afghan villages, nomad camps, and most urban areas ... would be almost unrecognizable to a sophisticated Muslim scholar," says scholar Louis Dupree. "Aside from faith in Allah and in Mohammad as the Messenger of Allah, most beliefs relate to localized, pre-Muslim customs." [5]

---

5 Dupree, *Afghanistan*, 104.

The Constitution of 2004 proclaims Afghanistan to be an Islamic Republic. Afghans affirm Muslim doctrines when they hear them. However, they may not hear them very often, or understand them when they do. Instead, the average person is preoccupied with the unseen forces that are teeming around. *Jinn* and ghosts, beautiful women fairies, giants and "shaitans" may show up anywhere. Particularly they inhabit gardens in springtime. They can cause sickness and misfortune. Sometimes they steal girls away. So a reasonable person will invest in magic, charms, and divinations as much as in orthodox religious rituals. There are many spells to avert the "evil eye." Cloth is tied on trees near saints' graves, and offerings are made in hope of good fortune—a pregnancy, a healthy child, a safe journey, graduation from school, protection against all kinds of evils.

This is the opposite of what Muhammad affirmed. It is what the fundamentalists are fighting against. But it remains widespread, partly because people have not been taught much about their religion and partly because Allah is too high and the classic Muslim rituals and disciplines are too formal to serve peoples' urgent needs. Afghans are desperate for a God that they can access right now.

Afghan Singularity

Most Afghans are fiercely Muslim. A new ruler always has a mosque sermon read in his name. An insult to Islam is taken personally. An enemy is called a *kafir* or heathen. If people oppose an idea or proposed law, they may label it "un-Islamic" even though it has nothing to do with religion.

Yet Afghans do not like to be subordinate to anybody, not even to God. "Only when the dagger is over his head does God enter his heart."[6] *Pashtunwali* may contradict *Sharia* law at some points, such as rights given to women, or punishments for certain crimes, or the *jirga* system of government.[7] In those cases, Pashtun Afghans believe *Pashtunwali* is superior. It is a purer code of ethics. Other people may need to follow Sharia, but Afghans have something better.[8] After all, Afghans have been Muslims for many centuries. They are secure in their religion and do not need to attend to the details as closely as new converts might. Afghan Islam constitutes a way of life, not a set of beliefs, they assert.

Sunnis, Shias, Ismailis, Sufi mystics and fundamentalist reformers like the Taliban and ISKP all are parts of the Islam of Afghanistan. Flowing deeper still is the spiritism and magic of folk Islam. Yet specific doctrines may remain vague to many people. What can they agree on? They believe in God: that is as basic as breathing. They believe in the centrality of the prophet Muhammad. They believe that morality matters. They believe that community is essential,

6 Ahmed, *Mataloona*, 21.
7 Ahmed, *Pukhtun Economy*, 295.
8 Anderson, *How Afghans Define Themselves*, 281.

and that the Afghan heritage (or perhaps their specific people's heritage) is a source of pride. And they believe that supernatural help must be accessible in a crisis. These are the simple touchstones that are important.

One more glimpse of Afghan religious life appears in *The Lightening Sky*, the biography of a modern, internationally-oriented man named Gulwali Passarlay. Passarlay has political aspirations, so what he says must be taken with a grain of salt. He also is young and like youth worldwide tends to redesign his religion to fit his desires. Still his reflections and longings offer another Afghan perspective on Islam.

Passarlay was thirteen years old when his mother sent him out of Afghanistan to prevent his being conscripted by either the government army or jihadists. Though he did not speak any non-Afghan language, he had to negotiate his way in the company of changing sets of rough adult men across Afghanistan, Iran, Turkey (three times, back and forth), the Aegean sea, Greece, Germany, France, and the English channel, and finally defend his request for help against the objections of hard-nosed interrogators in Britain.

One evening in England Gulwali has a nightmare. He feels evil presences and is tempted by suicide. He concentrates on breathing.

> Trying in vain to quiet the voices at war in my head, I turned over. Slivers of sunlight poked through the top of the window and with them came a sudden kind of comfort, a slow-dawning realization: *jihad*. Slowly I took out my Quran, turning through the pages reverentially, just as my father and uncles had taught me, searching them desperately for the absolute word of God, written for the day of judgement. I turned to the relevant pages.
> "You shall spend in the cause of God; do not throw yourselves with your own hands into destruction. You shall be charitable. God loves the charitable" (2:195).
>
> "You shall resort to pardon, advocate tolerance, and disregard the ignorant" (7:199).
>
> For the first time I truly understood what it means. Not the most manipulated, twisted concepts of *jihad* as "holy war." That's the false version used by terrorists acting in the name of Islam to commit terrorist acts, aimed at the indiscriminate killing of innocent people. The literal meaning of *jihad* is "struggle" or "effort"—the holy war within oneself. That's the battle I had been warring with myself all this time, the confusion and pain that had been crippling me since I had fled Afghanistan. And I understood now … it is a fight we must all fight in different ways—whatever faith we may come from or if we have no faith at all. That day, as the sun continued to fill my room, I knew beyond all doubt that I need my *jihad* so that I can go on loving. I fight *jihad* to be.[9]

---

9 Passarlay and Ghouri, *Lightening Sky*, 350–51.

Four Gospel Bridges to Muslims

For thinking Afghan Muslims like Gulwali Passarlay who long for something more, or for simple shepherds who are seekers, there are themes in their own faith that might point them toward the Lord Jesus Christ. Here are four such themes.

The Mercy of God

Every day in their prayers Muslims speak of the mercy and compassion of God, *al Rahman, al Rahim*. God is not merely a distant force. God is not just a severe judge. No, God showers us with good things like the beauties of nature, the warmth of family and community, and the revelation of his truth through prophets and Scriptures. God cares about us and pays attention to what we do. This is what Muslims believe.

Yet what a pale shadow this is compared to the mercy that comes to us through the Lord Jesus Christ. In Jesus we see God's mercy extending far more radically than we could have imagined. According to John 1:1–14, the eternal Word of God took on human form and lived among us. This is the great mercy of God—not only to create the universe and hold it all together, not only to maintain human history to its final conclusion, not only to communicate with us through prophets and Scriptures and the designs of nature, but most of all the mercy of God is expressed when God comes close to us in the person of Jesus, enters into our human vulnerability and pain, offers Himself in sacrifice, and then breaks free from death and steps out of the grave alive. This is amazing mercy, and it is the kind of mercy we need. An Afghan believer, murmuring *al Rahman, al Rahim*, may thank God for all his mercies, but most of all for the full mercy expressed in Jesus Christ.

The Substitutionary Lamb

One of Islam's biggest annual feasts commemorates something that happened to Abraham (Ibrahim). God asked Abraham to sacrifice his son. People at that time did practice child sacrifice occasionally, so Abraham prepared to do that. Then God intervened with a substitute sacrifice. To this day, Muslims from Qatar to Australia to France to Nigeria shop for a ritually-slaughtered sheep or other animal and take it home for a big family feast. As they celebrate, they remember God's care for Abraham when he provided a substitutionary lamb. In many places this event is called the Id al-Adha.

What happened to Abraham's son points to Jesus. In the gospel, Jesus is called the Lamb of God. The gospel says he died so that we human beings do not have to pay for our evil. He died in our place. God provided a sacrifice by becoming the sacrifice.

But death could not hold him. God absorbed death into himself and burst right out of it. God made death insignificant. Truly God is great, as Muslims continually affirm. God is so great that he not only conquered death but also passed right through it. And this God, stronger than death, is also self-sacrificing, tender, vulnerable, and loving. A seeker can meditate on this glorious mystery, rooted in a traditional feast but extending far beyond it.

The Bedrock "I Ams"

Every human being craves something to eat. When we come home at the end of the day, basic food is what we grab for—bread or rice or potatoes or yams, depending on the culture. In Afghanistan daily bread is almost a necessity. It is inexpensive, it is filling, it smells like home, and it gives comfort.

The Lord Jesus identified himself with this humble human longing when He said, "I am bread" (John 6). This is one of the seven "I Am" statements in the Gospel of John:

- I Am the Bread, ch.6
- I Am the Light, ch.8
- I Am the Door, ch.10
- I Am the Shepherd, ch.10
- I Am the Resurrection, ch.11
- I Am the Way, the Truth, and the Life, ch.14
- I Am the Vine, ch.15

Lilias Trotter was an artistically gifted Christian witness who lived in Algeria from 1888 to 1928. There she discovered that local Sufis were touched by Jesus's picture language. So she wrote and illustrated an Arabic-language book titled "The Way of the Sevenfold Secrets." It explored Jesus's seven "I Am" statements. This book was treasured and much discussed by the Sufis.

What could be more ordinary than bread? Or light? Or a door? Or a vine? Every human being requires light. Every person relies on vines or plants for food. Everyone needs to find a door of access at some point. Everyone wonders about life and death: is resurrection ever possible? Everyone reaches out for direction, a way that is true, and for empowerment, a life that is renewable. Jesus tapped into these bedrock human desires and then proceeded to unfold layer upon layer of meaning within them. Just as his picture language reached Arab Sufis, it can touch Afghans' imaginations and hearts.

The Righteous Citizen

What builds a good society? Protests explode on the hard stones of city squares across the Muslim world. Young people demand justice and righteousness from their officials. They condemn corruption, favoritism, inept policies and shoddy practices. Thoughtful Afghans echo this yearning.

Where can citizens of character be found, who will continue fairly and faithfully year after year and decade after decade? Afghanistan's greatest leadership models may be the prophet Muhammad and Alexander the Great. Both of them went from victory to victory, piling up power. Yet how sorely Afghanistan needs servant leaders. Some Afghans, reading the gospels, find a model in Jesus. He kept the law, spoke truth to power, crafted compassion creatively, and truly loved the people, to the point of laying down his life. Afghans are hungry for leaders like that.

The mercy of God, the substitutionary lamb, the I Ams, and the righteous citizen are four themes that start where Afghan Muslims live and move toward the Lord Jesus Christ.

CHAPTER 7

How to Bless Refugees

When Afghan refugees arrive, how can people help them?
Two families' stories—Rashid's and the Smythe's—show some
ways to bless these newcomers.
Escape from Afghanistan, reasons for the disaster, and God's
power through it all; what refugees need first; a church tutoring
program and a network of agencies; volunteers, critics, and
creative strategies.

Rashid was afraid. In fact he was desperate. This was the hardest moment he had ever faced. In August 2021, when the American forces left Afghanistan, when the Afghan president fled and the radical, fundamentalist Taliban took over, his family was suddenly in danger. He himself was in the US, where he had been studying and now was working. But because of his work with the former Afghan government and his Christian faith, his wife, son, and daughters were at risk of persecution.

They needed to get out.

Becoming Refugees

Leaving home is not what most people want to do. Of course, there are exceptions: students, adventurers, and others who are stuck in dead-end jobs or relationships may hanker for a change. But
most people treasure their everyday friends and
extended family, their local coffee shops and
markets and soccer teams and foods and
festivals. They would like to hold onto
their language and their heritage.
Leaving home hurts. Still, millions
have made that exodus and
now survive outside their
birth countries.

A good portion of these are refugees—people who have fled from danger. The UNHCR estimates that there are 82.4 million forcibly displaced people at present, with 26.4 million classed as refugees.

Rashid's family plunged into that stream. Slipping out of the city where their ancestors had lived for hundreds of years, where they had grown up, and where their lives were rooted, they piled into a bus and bounced and rattled for seven hours over four hundred miles to the Kabul International Airport.

Unfortunately, the city of Kabul was in chaos when they arrived. The situation at the airport was a disaster. After the Taliban took over, people panicked. Remembering the Taliban's harsh rule in the 1990s, ordinary citizens feared what the future would look like under that regime now. Masses from different provinces rushed to the airport, hoping to fly out. Sadly, it was not possible to evacuate more than a small percentage of the clamoring crowds. Tens of thousands, including Rashid's family, were left behind.

In touch with the news, Rashid could picture his wife and four children all too well. On the screen he saw moms and dads carrying children and even infants as they struggled to make their way to the gateways leading to the planes. "How can my precious family break through that huge throng?" he wondered. The clock was ticking. He was feeling more desperate every hour.

But "although I am still learning and growing as a young Christian, God has taught me that 'what is impossible with man is possible with God,'" Rashid says.[1] "That was our only hope. Even before I came to Jesus I looked to God as a refuge. And God has miraculously worked in my life to bring me to this point."

Human history has demonstrated cycles of falling and rising, suffering and joy, desperation and relief. Since the beginning when God created this world, humans have been tested with different challenges—from Adam and Eve to Cain and Abel to our own choices to accept God's wisdom or our own. These tests and challenges have made it obvious that humans are prone to err. But the good news is that Jesus came to this world to pass the test on our behalf and to prove to us that we as humans can and should rely on God's wisdom which offers us endless love, grace, and forgiveness. God also offers us an unending source of hope, especially when we are falling, suffering, and desperate.

It is exactly in these frightening moments that humans more than ever seek wisdom from God. And God answers. In these desperate instants, when people plead with God to show them a way, God often opens doors and brings others into their lives to help them deal with their situation. Admittedly, we are not always miraculously helped and rescued. Sometimes, despite seeking wisdom, people remain in difficult situations and in some cases never find a way out.

---

1 Luke 18:27.

Yet as Christians we believe there is a reason behind even this. The followers of Jesus trust that God is involved in every stage of our lives and plans ahead of us and for us. If a door is closed, it means that God will open another door down the hall. It is with this mindset that believers in Jesus live their lives: God is the source of love, grace, forgiveness, and hope.

When Rashid's family was careening around Kabul, pushed here and there, he was afraid. Then, when 120 innocent Afghans who were just trying to leave the country were annihilated by an explosion, he feared even more. At the same time, he remembered many examples of how God had revealed himself in the lives of humans and opened doors for them. He held tight to hope in the God of possibilities.

Afghanistan exemplifies a situation where most people have been living in a desperate state for a long time. All countries display political, economic and social problems, even nations in the "developed" world. In the US, for example, the recent surge of homelessness, unemployment, and the rising awareness of racial and social discrimination and injustice cripples our communities. Yet such challenges are more severe in poor, underdeveloped countries. Suffering is routine in those nations. Some appear to be failing continually. A useful measuring tool is the United Nation's *17 Sustainable Development Goals*. This targets some of the challenges, including extreme poverty, hunger, illness, gender inequality, low level of education, unclean water, polluting energy, and so on. While in recent years efforts have been made to tackle these problems, the global COVID-19 health pandemic smashed improvements back down into the dust. Millions of people continue to fight just to survive.

This was Afghanistan's situation. Then, to make matters worse, in 2021 the government fell into the hands of the Taliban. That shift of power had immediate consequences. The economy slid backward. Hunger and extreme poverty exploded. Massive starvation loomed. Meanwhile, religious, ethnic, and linguistic minorities increasingly were subjected to discrimination, oppression, and suppression. The population teetered on the edge of a humanitarian crisis.

Despite such difficulties, God's grace was and is the great source of hope for these people. Recent events show how God's invisible hand came to save the lives of many Afghans in miraculous ways. First there were twenty years of relatively peaceful development during the first two decades of the twenty-first century. Next came surprising help with evacuations when escape became necessary. More recently, there has been compassionate assistance for Afghans resettling in strange new places. Nor has God abandoned Afghanistan itself. God did not get on a plane and jet away. After all, God created the land and the people. Each Afghan person is a miracle, formed in God's image. Each one is the potential recipient of the power generated by Jesus's dying and rising.

God cares, and God remains in Afghanistan right alongside the local people who must chart a new destiny with whatever resources they have at hand. God will continue to work through both local and international personnel to bless Afghanistan.

One Family and God's Invisible Hand

As Rashid was pacing and crying out to God for his family, he remembered this message:

> This is what the LORD says: "Don't let the wise boast in their wisdom, or the powerful boast in their power, or the rich boast in their riches. But those who wish to boast should boast in this alone: that they truly know me and understand that I am the Lord who demonstrates unfailing love and who brings justice and righteousness to the earth, and that I delight in these things. I, the Lord, have spoken!" (Jer 9:23–24 NLT)

This verse of the Bible displays God's providence, which includes sovereignty (God is in control), omnipotence (God is infinitely powerful), predestination (God is in charge of how everything turns out), omnipresence (God is present everywhere and involved in everything), omniscience (God knows everything, is wise, and makes no mistakes), love (God is love and has the best interests of his children at heart), and justice/righteousness (God judges men and angels).

This text was the cornerstone for Rashid's conviction that God intervenes in our lives. Not only is God involved with believers, but also with unbelievers. There are circumstances when God's providence affects both. For example, God saves people from catastrophic events, whether a car accident or airplane crash or extreme poverty, hunger, or violent conflict. Sometimes God intervenes directly to show his omnipresence and omnipotence, and at other times indirectly, putting people in our lives who dramatically redirect us from falling, suffering, and desperation to rising, relief, and joy.

In Afghanistan, God blessed indirectly through people who helped after the fall of the first Taliban regime in 2001. Although the country is rich in resources and cultural heritage, it had suffered for centuries from external invasions and internal mismanagement. Beginning in 2001, however, Afghanistan started a new journey toward sustainable peace, stability, and development. This effort, supported by the international community and led by the United States, did put in place a relatively democratic government, which became a catalyst for some reforms and progress. God blessed through local and international people of good will and good sense.

Of course this progress was not comprehensive. It was relative. Sadly, even this did not last. Afghanistan yet again failed to keep to a stable path. Given its historical ethno-political, social, and cultural challenges, the new Afghan government constantly clashed with domestic power contenders. One of these was the Taliban movement. They led the insurgency against the government during the post-2001 era. Meanwhile, even as the government struggled with domestic challenges, the US decided to withdraw. Every Afghan and non-Afghan hoped this would be a peaceful transition. But it was not. The US withdrawal coincided with the immediate collapse of the Afghan government and the Taliban's abrupt return to power.

This sudden turn of events dramatically changed circumstances. Remembering the Taliban's brutality and oppression during their previous rule, fear overwhelmed many Afghans. They anticipated restrictive measures, punishments, religious extremism, and even persecution. While such negative experiences could happen to any Afghan, the ethnic, religious, and linguistic minorities, as well as those who had worked with the Americans or the government, were particularly at risk. So, as the Taliban returned to power, and the US started evacuating its officials and citizens and also Afghans eligible for immigration, Afghans in a panic suddenly streamed in from different provinces to storm the gates of Kabul International Airport. Within hours, tens of thousands of Afghans—those with and without documents to prove their connection to foreign countries—gathered around the airport, determined to find a way out.

International TV news showed women and men rushing to leave the country. Once again Afghans were experiencing suffering and desperation. While thousands did get evacuated between the 15th and 30th of August, tens of thousands remained behind, still desperately trying to leave their homeland, to find a haven somewhere in order to rebuild their lives. Among Afghans who were evacuated and those who are still waiting for a way out, there was a common refrain: "We initially had no hope, maybe because things happened so quickly, but then we realized that we should hope for the best. We turned to God for help. It was difficult to be hopeful, but we kept our trust in God."

God Blesses through People

God responded. God's invisible hand reached out to rescue many people, often by using others. In a very dramatic way, numerous organizations, groups, and individuals rose up to aid the Afghans. It seems that the God of the universe heard the suffering and desperation after the collapse of the government. When US forces withdrew on September 1st of 2021, and tens of thousands of Afghans still needed to leave the country, different organizations from across the world made possible the evacuation of more than 150,000 Afghans to the US and several European countries. Thousands more refugees now live in countries adjacent to Afghanistan while they wait for their immigration cases to be processed and approved.

Some US-based organizations that actively helped refugees find a way out of Afghanistan include Human Rights First, The International Refugee Assistance Project, Taskforce ARGO, Team Hope, The Lutheran Immigration and Refugee Service, World Relief, Keeping Our Promise, The International Medical Corps, The International Rescue Committee, Commonwealth Catholic Charities, The City of Fremont, and New American Pathways. These organizations helped with both evacuation and resettlement. Similar Canadian organizations include the Canadian government, UNICEF Canada, Islamic Relief Canada, and Veterans Transition Networks. Additionally, the Canadian government pledged to accept thousands of Afghan refugees in coming years. From the UK, Mercy Corps and Afghanistan Aid have been major sources of support for Afghan refugees. The UK government also promised to accept thousands of Afghan refugees in the years ahead. Some organizations have had more specific foci, like those supporting women or journalists. These include Women for Women International, Vital Voice, Georgetown Institute for Women, Peace and Security, and International Media Support.

It is quite amazing that so many organizations showed up. On short notice, these groups took Afghanistan as their main focus, gathered volunteers, and raised millions of dollars to support the Afghan people. Surely this was God's hand at work.

Task Force ARGO was one of these organizations. Unlike many, it was formed directly in response to the situation in Afghanistan. ARGO's mission was to bring home from Afghanistan every US Citizen and Legal Permanent Resident (LPR), the immediate and extended family members of US citizens and LPRs, and Afghan allies and partners who served the United States Armed Services faithfully as Afghan special operations personnel, interpreters, security specialists, and intelligence analysts.

The people behind ARGO were volunteers coming from Department of Defense, active-duty service members, veterans, current and former intelligence community members, law enforcement officers, elected officials, former special operators, intelligence analysts, military aviators, diplomats, defense industry executives, and subject matter experts.

ARGO took a well-planned, systematic approach. Long before getting people onto airplanes, ARGO prepared and coordinated the refugee families, tracking, shepherding, safeguarding, feeding, and housing them in Afghanistan while they waited for flights. In the end, Task Force ARGO assisted in evacuating thousands of Afghans. On their website are deeply appreciative comments. "Task Force Argo was getting the impossible done." "ARGO saved our lives." "My family was disappointed until my wife was contacted by a lady from Task Force ARGO." "Task Force ARGO has gifted me with a new life outside of Afghanistan." All in all, ARGO was like a rescue angel for these desperate people.

During this time, Rashid was crying out to God. He did not know how to help his family. They were at risk because of his work and his faith.

"Go to the international airport and get on a plane!" he told them over the phone.

But once they were at the airport, there was no plane free. Rashid was desperate, but he clutched God's invisible hand. He held onto hope in God's larger plan.

Because Rashid lived in the US, he also reached out to his state's leadership. He hoped to get some support from state senators so that his family would be included on an evacuation list. While exploring options, he found out that a staff member in one senator's office had a brother in the military with connections to an evacuation team.

Despite their efforts, there was not enough time to evacuate his family. Rashid thought that was it. But a couple of weeks later, "This guy reappeared almost out of nowhere. He called me and mentioned that there might be a chance for my family. 'Your family should leave in an hour,'" Rashid remembers. He could hardly believe it. That was a lesson to him: God's invisible hand rescues people in all sorts of ways. Later Rashid learned that the amazing Task Force ARGO was the instrument that God used to save his family.

What Refugees Need

Rashid's family is now safe outside Afghanistan in a holding camp in a third country. Before long they should be here with him. He cannot wait to be reunited with them. But then a whole new set of challenges will arise.

Providentially, agencies similar to those that helped people evacuate the country now help them settle as refugees. Often a local church or group of families will sponsor an Afghan family, backed by an agency like World Relief. The agency will deal with technical red tape while the church members tackle everyday details like tutoring school children, teaching local bus routes, explaining job applications, and generally hanging out as friends.

What are the areas where refugees may need help?

- Housing and Food
- Government Forms
- Language
- Job and Income (and financial education)
- Schooling for Children

- Health Care
- Transportation
- Internet (to communicate with family and friends in the home country and worldwide)
- Security (protection from crime)
- Life Rituals and Celebrations (funerals, weddings, religious events, life-transition ceremonies, community center, soccer, crafts, cooking, etc.)
- Changing Family Roles
- Trauma Healing

Most of all, refugees need the life-transforming story of Jesus. This story speaks to their profoundest longing. It is in Jesus that God has most fully revealed himself. It is through Jesus that people, whether poor or rich, find their deepest hungers met, find the truest prescriptions for health and healing. Jesus's story cannot be forced on refugees, but it can be offered regularly and spontaneously as a natural outflowing of God's love. It is a joy to share because it is what they need most of all.

Laura and Keith Smythe raised four children. When their family was grown, the couple looked at their big house and yard and wondered, "How will we fill this emptiness?"

Then Afghan refugees arrived. Through World Relief, the Smythes began welcoming a steady stream. First came Dr. Abdul's family. They had nine children. Dr. Abdul was a pediatrician, but since he did not have a US medical certification, he took a job as a translator. The Smythes had a finished basement big enough to take the whole family.

Before long World Relief helped the family move into an apartment complex, soon dotted with other Afghan families. But the Smythe and Abdul families have kept in touch. Laura and Keith were regular volunteers in the English as a Second Language program in the local elementary school, where they saw the Abduls' children.

"Can we come over and play in the yard?" the kids would ask. "There's no grass or playground at our apartment."

"Of course," the Smythes smiled.

"Would you honor us with a visit and take a meal with us?" Dr. Abdul invited. "We are so grateful for your hospitality." So the cycle of social exchanges continued.

More families arrived and stayed in the Smythe home. World Relief staff or volunteers took the newcomers to DSHS and Social Security offices, signed them up for health care, enrolled the kids in school, found them apartments, wrestled through the paperwork for their housing, and distributed donated furnishings. World Relief also has a roster of employers for entry-level jobs that do not require much English, like warehouses or factories, grocery stores or fish packers or construction. These are starter jobs while the immigrants settle in.

Without a sponsoring agency, all these steps become much more difficult. To rent an apartment, for example, a person needs a deposit and a record of a job and income extending over time. How can a recent immigrant provide this basic data?

But these are just the bare bones of survival. To thrive, people need community. They need to feel part of the society around them. To flourish in a new culture, people need to learn how to understand basic values and behaviors. Why do Americans just say "Hi, how are you?" and smile and rush on? Why do they pay so little attention to their parents and grandparents? Why do TV shows and videos imply that Americans are constantly changing sex partners? Why is "God" only a swear word? Certainly what newcomers learn through the media is skewed and incomplete, but sometimes that is all they have—unless real Americans like the Smythes will reach out and come alongside and share living spaces and mornings and evenings, even with leaky faucets and cranky kids.

Actually it takes multiple players to settle refugees well. A sponsoring agency like World Relief. A welcoming home like the Smythes. A school system that helps non-English-speaking students develop skills and understanding. Many of the Afghan kids speak no English when they arrive. The Smythes' church also became a base for volunteers and provided a bus and meeting places as needed.

One day when Laura was talking to the English as a Second Language teacher at the kids' school, the teacher lamented, "They'll lose so much over the summer!"

Laura went to her pastor. "Could we recruit volunteers to teach English classes over the summer?"

They hosted an invitational lunch, and thirty volunteers signed up. The regular ESL teacher was ecstatic. On Tuesday nights throughout the summer, the church provided classes in math and reading for the kids, English for the moms, and childcare for the babies and toddlers. The church also provided a bus to pick them up.

When the school year started again, Laura wanted to continue to do something for the moms. She went to the apartment complex supervisor and asked, "Could we use your club room?"

He was agreeable, but the little kids all accompanied their moms to English classes, and chaos reigned. Clearly, they needed to divide into separate groups.

Then they learned they could rent several rooms from the school district. It was within walking distance for these families. So one evening a week for three years that is what they did. And the program grew. Eventually they were using one room for parents, one for high school students, one for elementary students, and one for childcare. Even so, they ran out of space. So it was back to the church, where they used three buildings, as well as the church bus. Twenty volunteers showed up from the church, from World Relief, and from unexpected places.

Supporters and Critics

Meanwhile, a young Christian couple rented a unit in the Afghans' apartment complex, with an extra bedroom just to host new refugee families. Other Christians formed a HUB group, a community committed to long term relationships with Muslims. They sponsored a summer day camp called MegaFunFest. Besides dramatized Bible stories, the kids could choose tracks like construction, art, cooking, dance, gymnastics, and ball games. The group also began monthly barbeques in the summer, inviting three or four refugee families each time.

Partnering with another organization, they sponsored a Trauma Camp for Afghan, Somali, and Iraqi kids. Here children drew pictures or worked with crafts as they talked about some of the upheavals they had been through. Bible stories, especially stories from the life of Joseph, were a major thread. They also did trust-building activities to strengthen their confidence in others.

Keith likes to take groups of young teens on hikes in the summertime and snowshoeing in the winter. He also helps the dads and moms learn to drive so they can get their licenses. Laura has done marriage counseling with an upset Afghan wife, reading a book together and taking her to a church course on marriage.

For holidays, volunteers host celebrations or visit with cards and gifts. At Christmas and Easter, they write up a little story about why they celebrate this holiday. This past Christmas Laura decided to introduce the idea of Advent. She provided a goody bag and advent candles for each family, along with a note about how Advent starts a season when we thank God for his very special Gift.

At the Smythes, visits and new homestays continue. Sometimes things get broken. "Then we remember that our kids scribbled on the walls too," Keith says. "Hospitality means learning to let go," Laura adds. These newcomers will not be dependent forever. They are not intrinsically victims, just temporarily broken. But the friendships that have been built during this transition time are real and will last.

Not everyone approves this kind of involvement, however. Some sincere Christians may object, "Yes, we feel compassion. But we can't take in the whole world. We have problems already in our own country. Look at our homeless people. Don't they need food and shelter and jobs and trauma healing? Don't we have an obligation to help them first?"

These are valid concerns. But America has enough resources to absorb many more refugees. In fact when people are made aware of this challenge and opportunity, it often awakens their imaginations, stimulates creative ideas, and results in generating and multiplying new resources.

Jesus himself was an international refugee when Mary and Joseph fled to Egypt, escaping from Herod. To support the family, Joseph may have had to pick up odd jobs in a new country and struggle with directions in an unfamiliar language. Many biblical people had to move across borders—Abraham, Joseph, Moses, David, Daniel, Esther, Jeremiah, Ezekiel, Nehemiah, Ruth, and New Testament believers who fled persecution, like Philip and Peter and John. Remembering that heritage, we see that it is a privilege to be able to extend compassionate care to those who are vulnerable in this way.

Volunteers and staff can burn out, however. Sometimes the challenges seem unending. The problems may be too complex. Eventually a numbing "compassion fatigue" can set in. "To guard against this, (volunteers) must cultivate friends, social support, and religious support. They must set boundaries, including boundaries for media and for quiet time. They must give themselves space to feel pain.

> If possible, even amid overwhelming paradoxes, they must seek to make meaning out of their situation. Bathing in Scripture will help. On one hand, they can identify with many biblical people who faced incomprehensible circumstances, like Habakkuk. On the other hand, they are reminded that God himself entered human pain deeply through the incarnation and the crucifixion. And God ultimately will overwhelm all that causes tragedies, and will invite them into a glorious kingdom. Meanwhile, they can receive daily grace and empowerment to serve human needs, following God's own example.[2]

God's Hand and Human Hands

"God's grace rescued my family from danger," says Rashid. "Whatever lies ahead for us and other refugees, as well as for those who remain in Afghanistan, I believe God's invisible hand will be at work."

Through evacuation teams, refugee resettlement agencies, and true Christian believers, God has been helping Afghans find a safe refuge and take

---

2 Adeney, "Place Called Home," 17.

root in new communities. Often God uses the hands of ordinary people like Keith and Laura.

Driving past their house today, a person might be surprised to see a large colorful carpet dripping with suds in the driveway. Carpet weaving is a national skill, and Afghan women take pride in it. When they move to America, they buy traditional style carpets to place on top of the generic beige wall-to-wall carpets in their apartments. Once a year they want to wash their carpets, usually before one of the traditional *Id* festivals. But where can they wash these large rugs? There is no area big enough anywhere near their building.

Then they remember that the Smythes have a spacious sloped driveway.

So the hose comes out, and a carpet-washing schedule is set up to serve multiple families, because the washing and drying will require three (rainless) days. Cars, on the other hand, can be washed quickly. Since many Afghans drive Uber routes, they too pull in to make use of the tarmac, and to experience God's hand at work holding a hose.

CHAPTER 8

When Church Is Dangerous

No one is an island. Jesus's people need community. This chapter explores how Afghan believers find that community through internet churches, house churches, majority-culture churches, mature independent churches, godly marriages, and godly child raising.

"My daddy loved Jesus," says Balbas, a young man in Europe. "We were an ordinary Afghan family. Nothing particularly unusual about us. But somehow my daddy encountered the Lord Jesus and his people and his Word. He became passionate to share this good news. Something propelled him. So when he got access to Dari language Bibles, he made them available to business contacts and neighbors and really anybody who wanted one. Our region was of little concern to the government. For a year or two there was no trouble over these Bibles."

Then one day a Taliban delegate came to the door. "No more spreading of Christian Scripture is allowed," he mandated. "You have been warned."

But Balbas' daddy couldn't stop. He kept right on sharing the good news.

Three weeks later, he did not come home.

"Where's Daddy?" the children clamored at the end of the day.

"Maybe the bridge broke down," their mother answered, with a tense look on her face as she stirred the evening meal. "Maybe somebody wanted to talk more about God, and asked him to stay over. Or maybe he made a side trip to get supplies. Or maybe … " She stared off into space.

Balbas' father never came home again. In time they heard that he had been killed, but nobody ever found his body.

Wiping his tears, nine-year-old Balbas vowed, "I'm going to do what Daddy did." He started taking Bibles to neighbors. Soon an official note of warning arrived.

"Time to leave!" Balbas' mother declared. They fled Afghanistan. In Europe they found a good church. Balbas is now eighteen years old, and still inspired by the example of his father.

When church is dangerous, what do people do? "It is impossible to live openly as a Christian in Afghanistan," according to the *2022 World Watch List* produced by Open Doors. "Leaving Islam is considered shameful, and Christian converts face dire consequences if their new faith is discovered. Either they have to flee the country or they will be killed. This was true before the Taliban takeover. The situation has become even more dangerous for believers this year.

"If a Christian's new faith is discovered, their family, clan, or tribe has to save its honor by disowning the believer, or even killing them. This is widely considered to be justice. Alternatively, since leaving Islam is considered a sign of insanity, a Christian who has converted from Islam may be forcibly sent to a psychiatric hospital."[1]

But "the Word of God is alive and active … it judges the thoughts and attitudes of the heart" (Heb 4:12). When a person discovers that God in Jesus can transform his or her life, this is good news. This Word cannot be stopped. It seeps through barriers and jumps walls. So Afghans are coming to Jesus.

Some are led by a dream or vision. Others encounter a word of Scripture or a Jesus-follower. Or they may absorb the Good News through the internet or radio, or hear it from friends or relatives who have migrated to different parts of the world.

Private faith is not enough, however. We need each other. Jesus emphasized community, particularly in John 17. Muslims emphasize this too, referring frequently to the *ummah*, the body of believers. Community matters. How are Afghan followers of Jesus building this today? Four ways will be explored in this chapter.

Internet Churches

"Anybody want to talk about Jesus?"

Amin lives in a Muslim-majority country in Southeast Asia. He regularly enters chat rooms with this question: "Anybody want to talk about Jesus?" Hostile responses zap back. Yet not everyone who responds is negative. Some are thoughtful and open. Some welcome dialogue from a new perspective. Some truly want to know God personally. Amin has developed twenty long term relationships with inquirers through this simple question.

In Afghanistan there are WhatsApp churches and Facebook churches. Here believers can gather virtually to discuss a passage of Scripture. Internet security is tight, but there are ways around it. Inquiries about Jesus arise every day in

---

1 Open Doors. "Afghanistan," 6.

Afghanistan. Meanwhile, in the providence of God, there are Pashtu and Dari language social media teams on six continents who are at work responding back to these seekers.

Next door to Afghanistan, in Pakistan, there is a new internet outreach in Urdu language called PAK-7. With a population of more than 200 million people, Pakistan is one of the biggest countries on the globe. Worldwide it is estimated that there are 340 million Urdu speakers, including millions of Afghan Pashtuns who live in Pakistan or travel there.

PAK-7 has trained thirty Pakistanis as program-creators so as to broadcast the good news of Jesus through attractive formats. Some are dramas for the general market, in which Christian characters contribute to the good of society. Since most Pakistanis and Afghans have a negative view of Christians, this reframes their understanding. Other programs are for the Christian community, who need encouragement and teaching. Still other efforts target social media, like Amin does in Southeast Asia. These social media encounters raise questions and probe common hopes and fears and frustrations. Here Jesus is introduced as the powerful Savior who can give us wisdom and deliverance and cleansing and meaning and motivation.

In the Middle East, SAT-7 is a similar internet outreach. While it broadcasts primarily in Arabic, there are also programs in Farsi and Dari, Iranian and Afghan languages. SAT-7 is one of numerous internet ministries serving Iranians. For example, there is an Iranian pastor in Raleigh, Virginia who hosts weekly online Farsi-language worship for believers and seekers around the world. Afghans are some of those who join his fellowship.

Digital ministry, as well as radio ministry, can witness to people who have never heard the story of Jesus's death, resurrection, and transforming reign. It can interact personally and repeatedly with their questions. It can disciple new believers. It can systematically teach Scripture. It can provide worship services, including music and prayer. It can connect listeners and viewers to real people on the ground. It can help people access their own copies of printed, audio, or video Scripture portions. It can offer theological education to more mature followers.

But the internet is not enough. Online communication must be supplemented by face-to-face encounters wherever possible. During the COVID-19 pandemic, many of us experienced church worship online. How we longed to meet in person once again. Real life is not virtual. God has shaped us with bodies and set us in a wonderful material world. We will always need a touch, a smile, a cup of coffee, the aromas of our favorite foods, and a chance to kick a soccer ball around on a neighborhood field. Living online is not enough. The normal Christian life is local as well as global. Wherever possible, internet messages must be reinforced by bodily personal fellowship.

House Churches

For security reasons, we cannot say much about churches inside Afghanistan at this time. By "churches," we mean committed gatherings of believers, not official buildings. Any churches in the country are "house churches," secret because of persecution.

"The Afghan church lives with the daily awareness of suffering and persecution," says one leader. "Any day may be your last day. If the government doesn't kill you, your family or friends may, if they learn about your faith. At a minimum, you will lose your house and your job, and become an exile in your own country." A person who leaves the Muslim faith is termed an "apostate." His marriage can be invalidated. His children may lose their clan inheritance and may be blocked from education and jobs. Some Muslims believe that *Sharia* law commands them to kill apostates, particularly those in their own family. "So you share the gospel only in well-developed relationships with people you have gotten to know," this leader adds.

Afghan Christian suffering is tragic, yet it also models Jesus. In his sacrifice for us, Jesus endured shame, scandal, humiliation, and abandonment. This is at the heart of the gospel story. Every time Christians practice the fundamental rite of the Lord's Supper, they "proclaim the Lord's death until he comes" (1 Cor 11:26). It is not just resurrection, triumph, and glory. "The crucified wretch was pinned up like a specimen,"[2] cast out with a curse, numbered with transgressors, unjustly and grossly condemned, apparently godforsaken. Afghan Christians in their suffering may be closer to Jesus than many other believers around the world today.

It is in this context that the gospel is shared, and families like Balbas' come to faith. House groups are quiet but alive. Online resources nurture them. One network reports eighteen leaders-in-training who have been studying Luke, Acts, Genesis, Exodus, and Romans for a year and a half. In rotation, each student presents a couple of text-based lessons online, so they learn by doing as they develop habits of Bible study and teaching.

One student introduces his lesson on Acts by saying, "With my weak tongue and pen, I consider myself one of the servants of Christ from the bottom of my heart, and I ask God to grant me success to be one of the evangelists of God's Word and the good news of salvation in the place that God wants."

He continues: "Especially when the Taliban are brutally committing atrocities, most people are aware that they need to be saved from the current situation ... We ourselves want to be clear examples, showing that in these difficult political and social conditions God has touched our hearts and we have received the good news."

---

2 Rutledge, *Crucifixion*, 92.

On Paul, he comments, "Studying Paul's life makes us wonder that God gives good news to a religious extremist who kills innocent women and children, and touches his heart and allows him to enter heaven. We don't consider terrorists and criminals worthy of salvation. But God's grace is greater than we can imagine."

During this session, a military man happens to be sitting nearby. He begins to cry, and asks, "Is there any hope for me? I've committed inhumane acts."

So the gospel continues to speak in Afghanistan.

Another group emphasizes teachings about God, prayer, Christians, and the Bible. God is different from the traditional understanding of Allah. Prayer is not rote memory at set times, but personal conversation in our own words at any time. Christians are not drinkers and sexually loose like Western videos portray, but are people who follow the Scripture and bear good fruit. For example, Christians do not lie. This group encourages believers to read the Bible and raise questions about parts that they do not understand. For both of these ministries, most of the interaction occurs online first, and then proceeds to face-to-face.

Admittedly, it is difficult to verify such reports. There are a number of groups attempting internet ministry in Afghanistan. Seekers and believers may latch onto multiple ministries, and so may be counted multiple times in records. Some ministries give small amounts of money to support evangelism, to pay for tea or a simple meal. Naturally this may tempt people whose children are starving to appear more committed than they would be otherwise. Most reports are made in good faith, but there is room for error.

Next door in Iran there is amazing growth among Jesus's followers. The church inside and outside the country is said to be one of the fastest growing in the world. In spite of the fact that converts often are jailed, believers continue to multiply. The Iranian church may be a partial model for Afghans in years to come. Since governments and media security systems are always in flux, we may hope for more openness in Afghanistan in the future.

Unlike Afghanistan, Iran always has permitted some churches. These are "legacy" denominations of long standing, such as Armenian or Assyrian churches. Historically these church members' ancestors were Christians. By and large, the congregations are not composed of converts from Islam. Most of these churches worship in languages other than Farsi.[3]

By contrast, Iranian believers who are thrown in jail are those who convert from Islam, usually members of the majority Farsi-speaking population.

Whatever the language, the historic churches traditionally have welcomed inquirers from all backgrounds. Farsi-speaking people have attended, and many

---

3 Makarian, "Today's Iranian Revolution," and Adeney, *Kingdom Without Borders*, 148.

have believed. In time, since Farsi is the main language of the country, it was natural to switch to worshipping in that language. That provoked persecution, however. During the 1980s, repression increased. Several key pastors were arrested and executed. In 2008 government intelligence agents infiltrated a network of fifty churches, posing as sincere seekers. Church members were rounded up and forced to sign documents limiting their future association. Gradually the government closed all Farsi-speaking churches.

At that point, the congregations shifted to being house churches. Since then, in addition to those worshippers already present in Iran, many more house churches have been planted by leaders in exile who continue to support ministry inside the country. A low-profile approach called DMM (Disciple-Making Movements) was introduced in 2005 and now reports thirty thousand believers. Many of these grassroots Christians never have set foot in a church building. Beyond the borders of Iran, there are Farsi-speaking churches all over the world.

Majority-Culture Churches

Three of the ways that Afghan believers worldwide find Christian community are (1) online fellowships, (2) house fellowships, and (3) majority-culture churches. When Afghans migrate, they may meet Christians who invite them to church, whether they are in India or Brazil or Canada. Here some Afghans will discover Jesus as Lord, and some will be baptized. Here they may learn to read the Bible in the language of the country where they are living and learn Christian terms in that language. Even though they may be burdened by post-traumatic stress, economic problems, language challenges, and concerns about relatives back home, they still experience great blessing in the friendly fellowship and joyous spirit of the local church and find that their traumatized souls are refreshed.

Some churches will provide simultaneous translation for participants who do not understand the language well. For example, Village Church in Beaverton, Oregon provides sermons simultaneously in several languages. The English sermon is prepared in advance. ("The Holy Spirit must offer inspiration in the office," jokes the pastor.) This sermon is processed through a sophisticated translation system so that during the worship service people can hear well-crafted words and ideas in their own languages. The system has been developed by Kim-Fu and Chris Lim, Indonesian-American tech gurus.[4]

Joint worship services are not enough, however. When Afghans are part of a majority-culture church, that congregation should not only include them in all activities but also provide a place and time where they can enjoy a distinct fellowship of their own. Not all immigrants feel completely at home

---

4 This translation service is Spf.io/church.

in a majority-culture worship service. They long to cry out to God together in their mother tongue. They yearn to use distinctive "terms of address," some respectful and some endearing—Uncle, Sir, Elder Sister, Grandfather, son, daughter. It is a release, a joy, to mingle in a group where those terms pop up naturally in conversation. Similarly, it is a comfort to worship and pray with traditional gestures, movements of the head, the hands, and the body. Finally, migrants love to celebrate festivals and life events with familiar foods and music and humor and inside references to life back home.

Majority-culture churches can make a place for such fellowship groups. Various structures and degrees of integration are possible, taking into account money, authority, and decision-making as well as music, Sunday school, and parties. Unity as a framework for diversity is basic. A happy result will be a structure where youth can go back and forth between their dual heritages, all within the family of faith.

In reality, life is still more complex. Even if an Afghan group starts under the umbrella of one church, it may draw on a variety of streams. For example, one small monthly meeting includes Afghans who are members of two churches (of contrasting denominations), as well as friends associated with Cru, SIM, Open Doors, and an Iranian church. When life in the Spirit gives birth to unexpected connections, majority-culture churches must be flexible and continue to share counsel and collaboration.

Distinct men's and women's fellowship groups may be useful. In Afghanistan, people spend a great deal of time with others of their own gender, both for work and for relaxation and recreation. This feels natural. Conversely, some women might not feel comfortable speaking up in Bible study groups where strange men are present.

Further, many migrant Afghan men have greater command of English, literacy, and education than their wives. Gender-specific Bible study groups can be tailored to these realities. However, husbands and wives in Christian families also must learn to worship and study the Bible together. Both men and women are blessed by God's grace. Cultural courtesy may call for different role behaviors for husbands and wives, but these will evolve with each generation and location.

Mature Afghan Churches

Finally, beyond internet churches, house churches, and majority-culture churches, there are a limited number of mature Afghan churches. In Greece, for example, Masoud pastors a group of over one hundred Afghans. Growing up in Afghanistan, Masoud prayed regularly. Always sensitive to spiritual questions, he wondered about God and longed to be closer to him. When he travelled to

Europe and heard the good news of the gospel, he committed his life to Jesus. Korean missionaries in Greece discipled and trained him. Now he disciples Afghans, especially men.

When his congregation was just beginning, Pastor Masoud was mentored by Hellenist Ministries. More recently it has been supported by a Greek evangelical Presbyterian church. The members keep in touch with family and friends inside Afghanistan, sharing all kinds of news, including the gospel. However, the transience and fluidity of a congregation made up of refugees—people on the move—makes orderly and sustained church community challenging.

In North America some Afghan followers of Jesus gather for a conference annually, along with missionaries, refugee sponsors, and NGO and church representatives. Eighty Afghan believers joined this event in 2022. The meeting lasts for three days of worship and fellowship and encouragement.

While a few Afghan churches in the US and Canada may have twenty to thirty members, most are smaller house gatherings. Larger bodies may be joint efforts with Iranians. This Iranian-Afghan combination occurs worldwide, from California to Indonesia. In Turkey there are over fifty Iranian churches, many with Afghan members. Those Afghans who want serious Bible education may enroll in PARS, a premier Iranian theological education center based in England. This center also offers trauma care and counseling for persecuted Iranian and Afghan Christians. Another Iranian ministry, ELAM, includes Afghans in its leadership team.

Yet another Bible education program is the Afghan Bible College based in Turkey, with ten lecturers and fifty students, fifteen of them women. The students come from Pakistan, Germany, Iran, Turkey, and Afghanistan. Ten Afghan churches have been planted in Turkey through this ministry, and the students are actively discipling many Afghans back home.

Churches are not perfect, however. Wonderful as it is to worship and fellowship with others who love Jesus, heaven has not arrived. If Iranian churches are any model, Afghan churches may face certain specific stresses. In particular, fragmentation often seems to plague Iranian churches as they mature. Consider the Iranian church of Glasgow, Scotland. They report powerful prayer and fellowship weekly. Inquirers come seeking answers to prayer, and stay because they find truth and peace. Many immigrants have met the Lord here, and many lives have been changed. Still, "internal church crises have impelled people to leave the church at times … Generally, crises have started within the group of mature and committed members. Problems around arrogance, pride, and uncontrolled anger tend to come out … During one severe crisis last year, we had fewer than ten attendees for a while."[5]

---

5 Von Kaehne, "Iranian Diaspora Ministry," 445.

"[On the other hand,] reconciliation within this group, often preceded by genuine apology and humility, tends to be lasting. The love shown here is a very powerful witness."[6]

Given the fierce independence and competitiveness of many Afghans, it would be no surprise if fragmentation were to happen in their fellowships. After all, "the church is a bunch of sinners in one room," quips a young leader. All the problems of a young church may crop up. There may be conflicts over money, or leadership style, or ministry priorities, or simply favoritism—"you love them more than you love me." Social class and etiquette styles may differ. For example, in one of the first fellowships in North Africa, a strong woman leader complained that her greatest problem with the church was the mediocre quality of the cakes at church potlucks!

Tensions between Afghan ethnic groups may arise. Then, according to Ben Moradi, Matthew 28:18–19 applies: the gospel must be preached to all nations. That includes the other ethnic groups in Afghanistan. "We must grasp the big picture of salvation. It's not about me. They sin, yes. I sin, too. As I have been forgiven, so I must forgive, and recognize that the others are my brothers."

Thank God for internet churches, house churches, majority-culture churches, and fledgling, full-orbed Afghan churches. These are all containers for Christian community, for worship, fellowship, and service.

Marriage and Children

Families are the smallest building blocks of community. Before there are churches there are families: husbands and wives, parents and children, grandparents, uncles and aunts, brothers and sisters. Unmarried single people are parts of families, too, both families of birth and "adoptive families" made up of friends who share treasured, close, committed, long term ties.

We show our love for Jesus by affirming truths. We also show it through our actions. God gave us physical bodies and set us in social circles, telling Adam in the beginning, "It is not good for the man to be alone" (Gen 2:18). When we use our energies to care for others, we honor God. Excellent disciples nurture healthy relationships. This begins in the family.

Extended family members are some of the most important elements in an Afghan person's experience. When they need money or time, an Afghan pitches in. When they hold strong opinions, an Afghan sometimes stays quiet out of respect, especially for elders. It is true that quarrels and even fighting occasionally erupt. Still, the family, and by extension the local clan and tribe and community councils like *jirgas* or *shuras* are some of life's greatest riches.

---

6 Von Kaehne, 445–46.

Marriage

An Afghan disciple of Jesus must learn skills regarding marriage. In many traditional families, it is not customary for a man to discuss personal thoughts and feelings with his wife. Instead, he explores these with other men, whether kin or neighbors, often in informal groups. As a follower of Jesus, however, a husband discovers that he should love his wife as much as he loves himself, as much as he loves his own body, according to Ephesians 5. The text even says that a husband should love his wife like Christ loves the church. What does that mean? How is it possible?

While retaining the best of traditional role behaviors, the couple must learn to talk together, pray together, make decisions together, and work together as "heirs with you of the gracious gift of life" (1 Pet 3:7). Watching healthy Christian families will help. Also, believers in the same fellowship group can commit to encourage and pray for each other's marriages.

This issue arose in a country near Afghanistan where the Spirit of the Lord swept across thousands of Muslims, and they had turned to Jesus. The believers were mostly men. They were the ones who heard, responded, learned Scripture and Christian disciplines, and planned for the future of the movement. Women were not consulted. The men did not even consider that their wives would be interested or have anything to offer.

A foreign Christian woman consultant was brought in to help start women's craft projects. During one lunch, a local believer rather idly happened to ask this consultant, "Shouldn't I beat my wife?"[7]

She was horrified. "Of course you shouldn't." That night she texted him key Scripture passages on marriage. He and his friends stayed up all night discussing these. The next day they announced that they had made a commitment not to beat their wives anymore.

It was not easy. How else do you get a woman's attention? How else do you impress on her the seriousness of something? Habits were ingrained. Learning new communication patterns took time. But it was worth it.

God created Eve to be Adam's companion, not his servant (Gen 2:18). To build that companionship, a man must put his wife above his father and mother (Gen 2:24). Of course, he will honor his parents. But his wife has priority. Together the two of them must learn how to care for each other, how to talk together, and how to trust each other. *Come Follow Me*, a discipleship guide by Tim Green, has a fine chapter on husbands and wives, with basic Bible texts. This is available in Dari and Pashtu languages.

---

7 Garrison, *Wind in the House*, 198–203.

A particular marriage problem assails some refugee men. When they fled the country, they had to get out quickly. The journey ahead was unknown and dangerous, so they left their wives and children behind. Now they have settled into their countries of asylum. That might seem like good news. Unfortunately, it may be years before their families can join them, if that ever happens. What is marriage for such men?

Around them they may see happy Afghan families who managed to come out together or reunite later. Standing on the outside looking in makes these men feel more lonely and isolated. They are sheltered and fed, but nobody needs them here the way a family would. They also face sexual temptations. This difficult marriage situation is not unique to Afghans. It confronts asylees from many countries. Can the church acknowledge the problem? Too often even ordinary citizens who are single feel that they are on the margins of church life. How much more acute is the loneliness for those who have no roots here and hardly speak the language.

If these refugees were invited to help out in service projects, they might feel more significant. They might also find some joy in sports programs. While these activities will help, inevitably there will be days and nights of pain and confusion, calling out to God and asking, "Why?"

Children

The hope of the future of Afghanistan lies in the children. They are the investment of surpassing value. Traditionally it has been the responsibility of the extended family to train and discipline children. Members of the wider community, too, would feel free to comment and make critiques on a child's behavior. Potential shaming by older people does a great deal to modify the way a child acts. Yet to speak of a single child is misleading, because no child stands alone back home. Each child is surrounded by other children, siblings and neighbors, playmates and fellow explorers, and sometimes also rivals. Afghan children are noted for being fearless and feisty. Boys in particular may be treated like little princes. However, their peers, relatives, and community will shave off their rough edges and polish them into acceptable human beings. In this milieu it does take a village to raise a child.

All this changes when Afghans migrate. No longer are they surrounded by their extended family, their traditional community, or even the peer group of local children. If they have moved to the US or another Western country, they will encounter a different pattern for child raising. Here the nuclear family guides and disciplines the child.

Suddenly a very heavy responsibility falls on the shoulders of immigrant fathers and mothers. Usually they do not even realize what has happened: the duty of disciplining and training has landed solely on them. They probably do not recognize what they have lost—a great circle of role models and fellow disciplinarians—and the implications of this loss for the development of their children. In this vacuum, children will fill their minds with media messages. These will not adequately replace the human lessons they would have learned from the community back home, however imperfect it was.

Christian parents need to acknowledge this challenge. They must try to learn positive parenting skills. They should watch healthy families. Where possible they should build sustained relationships with another family or two. This may serve to some extent as an extended family. Within this framework several trustworthy adults can become models and can speak into the children's lives. Cultivating a "grandmother" or "grandfather" in the church can enrich children too.

A helpful book on raising godly children is *Child Raising*, available in Dari language from Afghan Media Centre. This is a downloadable "guide for parents on how to bring up their children in such a way that when they grow up they can play a positive role in society." Though only 62 pages, it is full of counsel on how to develop a Christian home and how to discipline, encourage, and motivate children.

Going beyond general nurture and training, Christian parents also must offer their children specific Christian teaching. When Moses gave the people their confession of faith, he commanded them to speak about it with their children (Deut 6). George Barna Research Group finds that "by age 13, one's spiritual identity is largely set in place."[8] According to this research, there is a 32 percent chance that children ages five to twelve will come to faith in Christ when they are exposed to the gospel, while there is only a 6 percent chance after age nineteen.

Although parents may not feel qualified to teach the Bible, at least they can pray and read—or listen to—the Bible as a family every day. Daily prayer is nothing strange for Afghans, who have been taught to recite memorized ritual prayers to a distant deity. Now as Christians they can lead their children in prayer to a loving Father.

Children also need focused teaching in the fellowship group. It is not enough for a home group to teach adults. Children running around or playing in the next room are missing crucial lessons. Valuable hours and months and years are being lost. However, this is a steep challenge for new immigrants. It seems like one burden too many. How can it be tackled?

The group can team up temporarily with more experienced leaders. A one-week Iranian Christian camp that took place in Vancouver in 2019 offers a model. Children between ages four and twelve were invited. Fourteen Iranian volunteers and seven experienced non-Iranians ran the activities.

---

8 Lausanne Movement, "No Unreached Children."

"We held a volunteer meeting the month before the camp to examine the Scriptural basis for children's discipleship as well as to explain the logistics of the camp. Iranian volunteers were paired with non-Iranian volunteers for several of the camp stations, which included Bible story, crafts, sports, and snacks. Non-Iranian volunteers led teams of children between the stations and conducted worship, Bible memory work, and science experiments during the morning and afternoon assemblies."[9] Pastors of the participating Iranian churches took turns giving devotionals.

For parents there was a station where they could enjoy snacks. Two Iranian volunteers were available to talk with them.

"We didn't realize we should be teaching our children," some parents commented.

In the following months and years, several similar children's events were held. The parents became comfortable with these activities. The sponsoring Iranian churches and pastors publicly expressed appreciation. Eventually the volunteers were all Iranian.

For overburdened Afghan immigrants, teaching children may seem like one more difficult task. At first they may want to collaborate with a majority-culture church to access volunteers and curriculum. If some volunteers speak only English, that is not much of a barrier for children, who adapt quickly. Over time Afghan adults increasingly can run their own children's teaching events. "Start children off on the way they should go, and even when they are old they will not turn from it" (Prov 22:6).

Family and friendship are the simplest building blocks of Christian community. Even though human connections between believers may be dangerous in some places, community remains essential everywhere.

Two Christian communities on two continents blessed the family of Dr. Karim on their journey. Here is their story.

Churches on Both Sides of the World

With a house worth $350,000 and a car worth $20,000, Dr. Karim had a very pleasant and comfortable life. After finishing medical school in Kabul, he ran a successful medical practice. Occasionally he lectured at his alma mater.[10]

But when his friend's head was chopped off and left in the center of the dining room table, Karim knew it was time to go.

Actually, it seemed like history was repeating itself. Two decades earlier Karim and his family had fled the country to escape violence and terrorism. Once they were settled in Pakistan, Karim had established a clinic. There he treated

---

9   DeLange, "Unpublished Paper," 2.

10   George and Adeney, *Refugee Diaspora*, 11–16.

Afghans who had escaped the country just as he had. Twenty years later, after the Russians left and the power of the Taliban declined, Karim and his family moved back home. There were new job opportunities. Karim worked for several NGOs connected with the United Nations. Though they did not offer pensions, they paid five to ten times more than the government. During those years Karim also studied further and became recognized as an ultrasound specialist.

Tragically, the Taliban revived. Life grew dangerous once more. Weapons left by the Soviets were added to weapons left by those who had fought against them. Although opium wealth oozed over the land, most people remained poor. Four million orphans, the leftovers of war, scrambled just to find something to eat. Young adults longed for a better life. When the Taliban painted a positive vision of the future, more youth joined them.

The Taliban objected to doctors like Karim working with foreign agencies. Some of his patients warned him about this because they appreciated his care. But Karim didn't take their worries very seriously. He had a good salary and a settled life.

Two nights after his colleague was beheaded, the Taliban came for Karim. They crashed into his house at 1:00 a.m. For an hour and a half they terrorized and tortured his family. He still cries if he starts to tell about it.

Leaving everything—his expensive ultrasound machine, the house, and the car—they fled to India. Once again they began to rebuild their lives. Karim carried a certificate from the International Medical Corporation. This qualified him to treat some patients, but not to open a clinic.

"I'm lonely here, Dad," his daughter said. "Can't we find some other Afghans?"

He began to ask around. That is how he discovered an Afghan church. Almost a hundred people worshipped together on Saturdays and Sundays. During the week there were Bible studies in different people's homes. They were warm and caring and outgoing and interested in Karim's family. And their view of life and spirituality was interesting. Karim began to take classes. "We were beginners in spiritual works, like how to pray," he says. "But I came to see that there was a way of living that was better than Islam. So I changed."

After they professed faith in Jesus as Lord, they took discipleship classes for two months. Then they were baptized. Previously in Afghanistan Karim had treated a few Christian patients. He had thought that Christianity was for super people, those who had a car and a good income. Now in New Delhi he saw that Jesus was for everybody. Ordinary Christians demonstrated joy and peace in spite of their refugee conditions.

This church had begun when Korean witnesses were expelled from Afghanistan. Two Korean women resettled in New Delhi and began reaching out to Afghans there. Four or five times a year teams from Korea would join them.

Today there are several strong Afghan churches in India. Karim found the members in his congregation to be honest, caring, and even fun-loving. "They were fellow Afghans, but different and a better kind of people. The only way to explain the transformation is their encounter with Jesus."

Eventually Karim's family moved on to the United States. Once more they were strangers. While the refugee welcome team was kind and helpful, the family missed their Indian church. Although it was after midnight in New Delhi, Karim phoned from Chicago. "I'm sorry to bother you at this late hour, but I missed church so much this Sunday," he told his friends. "Would you pray that we can find a church here next Sunday? How can we find one? We don't have internet yet. But God is the same God everywhere. Please pray."

Through his mobile phone he heard the brothers in India asking God to help him connect with some church in Chicago.

The next week Karim and his sons went shopping for household goods. "Bring back a clothes iron," his wife requested. As he walked down a store aisle, Karim spied a strange sight: a man was holding up an iron. He took the man's arm. "Excuse me. May I ask where you found that iron?" he questioned.

"Do you need an iron?"

"Yes, my wife wants me to buy one."

"You can take this one," the man said and handed it over.

"Oh no. You need it—"

That man turned out to be the pastor of New Hope Community Church. To Karim that was even more important than the iron. The next day Pastor Bob visited them. When he saw how dark their room was, he came back with a portable lamp. Then he drove Karim to the church so he could see how close it was.

Many Americans have been friendly to Karim's family, but meeting Pastor Bob was the best experience of all. "How marvelous it is to experience God's family in a new place," Karim says. "I had called my church in India and asked them to pray that God would show me the way, because I didn't know where to go. Then in the market, even though I knew it was discourteous to grab someone's arm, I did it anyway, and God connected us. God is the same God everywhere. By means of an object as simple as an iron, we found Christian fellowship in our new homeland."

Community is vital. We need places to fellowship and worship and learn and grow and be God's people together. Thank God for internet churches, house churches, mainstream churches, and full-orbed Pashtu or Dari speaking churches that are emerging in various parts of the world. Two of those churches, on two sides of the globe, made all the difference for Karim's family.

Chapter 9

Beauty and Worship

The beautiful expression of the soul in worship and witness occupies this chapter: Storytelling and memorizing, singing, celebrating, and praying.

Snakes as thick as your arm slither through this jungle. Spiders can drop on you. Salam swatted a clutch of mosquitos buzzing at the back of his neck. Did they carry malaria? Dengue fever? He sloshed through soggy weeds, and wet mud oozed around his toes.

This was the Darien Gap, ninety miles of nearly 100 percent humidity. Here the PanAmerican highway that supposedly runs from Alaska to Argentina just gives up. Darien is a narrow isthmus connecting the two great American continents. It is where the Spanish explorer Balboa first gazed on the Pacific. Today it is sometimes called "the most dangerous place on earth." Not only are there large wild cats in the trees and crocodiles on the ground, but human thugs of all kinds can crash out of the underbrush: crazy narcotics traffickers, Colombian terrorists, and sadistic national police, as well as wild lone rangers. There are no towns, no law, and often no trails. If you wander off or get injured, you are finished.

Why was Salam here? He had been living and working in Afghanistan, running a business and raising his family of five children. But when the Taliban came to power, his life was in danger and he had to get out.

Greens. Jade green, olive green, and teal green leaves and fronds swished past as Salam plodded on, dragging one foot after another. Wouldn't Picasso have loved these colors! And Van Gogh. And Monet. And Behzad, the miniature painter of Herat who created during the pinnacle artistic era of the 1500s, the years when exquisitely designed tiles, illustrated manuscripts, and miniatures flowed from Afghanistan to Persia and India and throughout the Ottoman empire.

Salam was a painter. Although he grew up in a poor family, he had talent. From an early age he drew and painted. After high school, he studied at the Vocational Educational Center of Behzad in his province. This institute is renowned for teaching calligraphy, drawing, painting, and general arts. Eventually Salam started a publishing business. It printed booklets, receipts and even large banners. Afghan and foreign companies hired him to paint designs on walls.

What varied leaf patterns there were in this forest, Salam observed as he trudged on. Some were five-fingered like hands, others long and narrow, others small and shimmering, others broad as plates, some drooping, others erect. If only he had a pencil or paintbrush and the time to stop and record these designs. Oops! Was that a snake wriggling across the grass just in front of his foot? Would he survive this death route?

Salam could not reveal to any of the others in this ragged group of refugees that he was a Christian, because they were Muslims and would have turned on him. He prayed silently, "God, You have helped me throughout my life. Help me now in this stage as well."

As he prayed, it seemed like God was paving the way ahead of him. Even as he dripped sweat and swatted mosquitos and sagged from weariness, he felt that God was telling him he would come safely through this danger. Jesus came into our world to save us from eternal death, and Salam sensed that God would save him from death on this journey now. That gave him the confidence to keep strong as he continued along the scary route.

When the Afghan government collapsed in 2021, Salam had fled. First he slipped out to Iran, just west of Afghanistan. After two months without a job or destination, he decided to switch directions. Crossing secretly back through Afghanistan, he emerged into Pakistan, the country on the east. After that it was no great distance to proceed to Qatar on the Arabian Peninsula. There Salam heard about Afghans who were living in Brazil. He had brought along enough money to make the flight to South America, so that is where he went.

Meanwhile, he was in contact with Christian friends-of-friends in the US. They invited him to join them, although they could not provide him with legal residence papers. He decided to try it. After seven months in Brazil, Salam began an arduous journey northward through ten nations. The route wound through Brazil, Peru, Ecuador, and Colombia. Then it spiraled north through the Central American countries of Panama, Nicaragua, Costa Rica, Honduras, Guatemala, and finally Mexico. Sometimes Salam took a bus or train. Sometimes he got on a boat. A couple of times he flew. Often he just walked.

Was this long journey necessary? Why did Salem leave Afghanistan? He had solid reasons. First, as a painter and artist, he had drawn pieces depicting the Taliban's brutal behavior against the women of Afghanistan. Second, he had run galleries and exhibitions for provincial reconstruction teams. These were sponsored by NATO. The new Taliban government would strongly condemn this foreign connection. Staying would put his life and his family's lives in danger.

The third reason Salam had to leave was that he was known as a friend of Christians, and in fact had become a Christian himself. There was an Afghan named Awaal who spoke widely about Jesus and had been inviting Afghans to follow the Lord. Many had responded. Awaal was imprisoned, and then had to leave Afghanistan. He went to Pakistan and was imprisoned there too. Eventually he went to Abu Dhabi.

Awaal and Salam were from the same province. Salam knew Awaal's brothers, and more distantly he knew Awaal himself. Salam was known for his artistic talent throughout the area, so Awaal was aware of him. It was natural that when Awaal had the opportunity, he shared the Good News of Jesus with Salam.

Salam was frustrated as a Muslim because he was not able to fulfill all the obligations of the religion. Even more important, he was not able to pursue his art fully. The religion discouraged paintings of humans and animals. It is believed that such representations could lead to idolatry. Abstract designs are better. Muslim art has excelled in those. But Salam found it maddening to be so limited.

"I started reading the Bible and talking to Awaal about it," Salam says. Awaal had given him a Farsi language Bible two years earlier. "Slowly I began to understand the differences between Islam and Christianity. The love of Jesus's followers also impressed and attracted me. I wanted to learn more. That is why I kept reading the Bible."

Today Salam says it is amazing to be directly connected with the God of the universe and talk to Him. This is very different from Islam. God's invisible hand has been holding him up in different stages of his life. In particular, it seems miraculous that he survived the very dangerous route from South America. Salam also is surprised by how God's people have come into his life, helping him resettle in the US and put down roots in a new community.

When he crossed the southern border of the US to enter the country, Salam registered as an asylum-seeker. Now he is waiting for an appointment with the government to review his case. He has no paying job. His wife and children are all back in Afghanistan and he cannot apply for them to join him until he has legal status here. He does not speak English well. He gets lonesome. He has discovered that not all struggles are physical ones like those on the death march through the Darien Gap. There are temptations and discouragements anywhere. Battles continue even in the land of plenty in America.

Salam does have some fellowship with American Christians and with a few Afghans. And he paints. In the long tradition of Afghan artists, he hopes to have a showing of his paintings before long.

Salam is part of a noble heritage: Afghanistan is the home of rich traditions of beauty. Gold, silver, blue lapis lazuli, intricately and imaginatively woven carpets and myriad other resources and art traditions have shimmered in this land for over four thousand years. Verbal and musical arts resonate too.

Worship often involves beauty. Beautiful words, beautiful music, beautiful material setting. From candles to ecstatic dances, from oratorios to drums, from psalms to intricate rhythms and gestures, beauty infuses worship. This goes beyond theology and church organization, important though those are. Worship is the sincere expression of the heart and spirit. When worship can be offered in community with our whole bodies, it is strengthened.

Worship to Jesus naturally should draw on the specific art traditions of the worshippers. Unfortunately, most Afghans' disciplers do not know this country's music or art. They turn unconsciously to generic Western-influenced world Christian music styles. In time these foreign songs may become precious to Afghan believers, associated with the love of God, the love of other Christians, and their own steps of growth.

Some Afghans do want to move away from their heritage, especially if they are living outside of Afghanistan. Those who are young may be impatient with traditional culture. Those who have suffered may desire to leave behind whatever reminds them of their trauma. Not all Afghan believers will share the same tastes when it comes to styles of worship. This is normal. Still, roots are not nothing. Cultivating a people's story down through the generations is a privilege. When it is done right, worship that connects with a heritage will add layers of richness and meaning.

In previous chapters we have explored religious beliefs and church patterns. In this chapter we consider stories and poetry and music and celebrations and prayer. These activities can draw our hearts and spirits and bodies into worship.

Storytelling and Memorizing

"Recite for us, Marion! Recite a holy story!" the women call out.

One of the regular Muslim celebrations is under way in Pakistan. Separate from the men, women have been sitting, chatting, and drinking tea for hours. If there is someone who is a good reader, she has shared passages of the *Quran* aloud. Though the women don't understand the Arabic words, they like the cadence of syllables that they associate with holiness and righteousness.

Marion can recite sacred stories in their own language, Urdu. During the years when she was becoming fluent in that language, Marion memorized many Scripture passages. Now, when the women urge her forward, she stands gracefully. She holds her hands out, lifts her face, smiles, and dramatically declaims a story from the Old or New Testament, or a psalm. The women are enthralled. The text comes to life as God speaks their language. Sitting on their mats, they are included in the grand cosmic epic, the never-ending story.

This story is foundational. Many good things occupy believers—organizing a church or fellowship, studying Christian disciplines, sharing the gospel with seekers, loving our neighbors. Underneath it all is the Bible, the word of God. This must be a priority. Other activities are energized when the whole Scripture flows richly through us. In the words of the Hispanic theologian Justo Gonzalez, "The purpose of our common study of Scripture is not so much to interpret it as to allow it to interpret us ... The lamp is a means to an end ... The final purpose of interpretation is to discover what obedience requires of us."[1]

Some Afghans come to Jesus because of a dream, a friend, or a prayer. They definitely encounter Jesus, experience the Holy Spirit, and enjoy life in a new dimension. However, they are hazy on beliefs and doctrines. They grasp only the fringes of the truth that Jesus is God. They are eager to know more, but there is a steep learning curve ahead. What is the larger story? What are the biblical foundations? What are the theological priorities? What are the implications for daily life? None of us grasps these basic truths completely. Naturally it will take time for a new believer to absorb teaching in these crucial areas.

An excellent discipling guide for Muslim-background followers of Jesus is *Come Follow Me*, compiled by Tim Green. This 20-chapter, easy-reading book is available in Dari and Uzbek languages and soon will be available in Pashtu. Distributers include the Afghan Media Centre in Canada and Word of Life Press in UK. *Come Follow Me* has an edition which meshes with the 2022 version of the Dari Bible, as well as an alternate which is adapted to the older Bible translation. It also has audio aids for oral learners. Each lesson suggests a practical application. Ideally this course is studied in dialogue with a mentor. Other Afghan-language print, audio, video, and digital Bible study aids are available from several sources.[2]

But Scripture is not just a theology textbook or a practical how-to manual. God gave us a story. Revelation is mostly narratives, poems, and letters—words set in distinctly human contexts. The cosmos begins with a Person who is active, wise, all-powerful, and impelled by love. There is evil. There is battle.

---

1 Gonzalez, *Manana*, 86.

2 Sources for Afghan language Bibles and Christian resources (print, audio, video, digital, phone apps, SD cards) include: Hope 4-Afghans, Pamir Ministries, Khabarkhush, Afghan Media, and Christar.

There is sacrifice. There is restoration, and empowering, and transformation, and a stupendous party. The story brings our theology to life. Through specific segments we learn general truths. Study and analysis will never be enough. Beyond rational investigation, we must inhale and mainline the story until it flows through us.

J. R. R. Tolkien, who created *The Lord of the Rings* trilogy, called the biblical epic a "eucatastrophe." What did he mean? Tolkien took the Greek prefix "eu" which signifies happiness and added it to the word "catastrophe." In fiction, Tolkien pointed out, two classic plot genres are tragedy and comedy. Tragedy is more significant. Its literary power packs a wallop. Yet when God in Christ went to the cross and rose from the dead, a truly joyful catastrophe unfurled. This was not a comedy but a grand cosmic tragedy birthing amazing new life.[3]

In this magnificent story, we see what God is like, what he has done for us, and what he will do. Afghans need to experience this as a unified narrative, not a set of separate anecdotes—not just Nicodemus, the woman at the well, Zacchaeus, etc. No, God is at the beginning of time and at the end. Bible stories must be set in that large framework, not doled out like pearls on a string. And, while "happily ever after" often is fake in our stories, it is real in eternity. Heaven wraps up the grand epic. Heaven is the finale, the dazzling party for people like Afghans who love parties but have lost so much. The story is not finished until we thrill each other with anticipations of heaven.

Memorizing and reciting the Scripture, like Marion does, can help. Muslims, Jews, Buddhists, and Hindus all speak their Scripture aloud. For Muslims, in the words of the scholar Kenneth Cragg, "the speech of God comes into the storehouse of memory and then into the currency of our lips."[4] Being invited to memorize Scripture feels normal and natural.

For forty years in a town in Pakistan, two foreign women operated a small clinic and told stories of Jesus. Hundreds of Muslims came to faith during those decades. Each new believer was directed to memorize thirty-four verses from the gospel of John. If they could not read, they learned orally from someone else. As a result, simple laborers came to feel that they *owned* the Good News: it was inside them and no one could take it away. With that confidence, they became flaming witnesses, and drew many others to Jesus.

Zaide is a simple Syrian mother. When a bomb wrecked her home in 2018, her family of seven fled to Lebanon. Although they were Muslims, a local church helped them with food and schooling. Zaide was invited to attend church and then to join a small group. Participants in that group received copies of Bible texts and were asked to memorize them.

---

3 Tolkien, "On Fairy Stories."

4 Cragg, *House of Islam*, 41.

"So I do," Zaide told me (Miriam).

"Oh? What verses have you memorized?" I wondered.

Immediately she responded (in Arabic), "'I have hidden your word in my heart, that I might not sin against you.' Psalm 119:11." Then she continued, "'Thanks be to God! He gives us the victory through our Lord Jesus Christ.' 1 Corinthians 15:57." She added, "Jesus died for us. He died for everybody. The cross is central to everything. I want to learn as much as I can so I can take it back with me when I return to Syria."

Even in her extreme situation, Zaide was bathing in Scripture, absorbing it, and letting it flow out naturally.

A believer might invite a seeker to memorize Psalm 1:1–3 together in Dari or Pashtu. "Why don't we take in a bit of sacred wisdom?" the believer might suggest. Then each time they meet, they recite the verses again. Psalm 1's appeal to righteousness and the beautiful image of a tree will delight Muslims as well as Christians. This can be a starting point, a springboard for committing many other texts to memory together.

Whether through memorizing or storying, through video or audio or face-to-face encounters, Afghan disciples must prioritize Scripture.

Singing

"Do not get drunk on wine … Be filled with the Spirit, speaking to one another with psalms, hymns, and songs from the Spirit," the apostle Paul advised when believers wanted to party (Eph 5:18–19). Afghans know the prohibition against alcohol. But what are songs of the Spirit?

A flute melody winds up against the jagged snowy mountain chain. A drum throbs in the bazaar, shades of tones alternating as fluid fingers give way to the flat palm of the hand. Tasting food from a pot over a fire, a woman hums a folk tune. Pacing along beside his sheep, a shepherd sings snatches of an epic. In big annual celebrations overflowing with crowds, all the instruments join, including eighteen-stringed lutes and *tambours*. This is grassroots music in Afghanistan.

When we sing or play an instrument, our whole body vibrates—mouth, chest muscles, hands and feet—and our emotions flow out. That is why the Psalms call us to praise God through song. It involves us totally. And music functions comprehensively, allowing us to worship, to teach, or to witness. Even where people condemn spoken testimonies, they are often spellbound when someone sings the gospel, and plead for more songs.

Afghan Christian worship songs are being crafted in refugee camps and elsewhere, and are circling the globe via the internet. These are simple songs. It is time for Christian ethnomusicologists to study the musical genres and instruments of Afghanistan, and join with gifted Afghans to create songs that pull together multiple dimensions, interweaving heritage music with music from the contemporary world.

This is more complicated than might be imagined, however, because traditional Afghans condemn music! Or so they say. Music is not Islamic, they believe. The Prophet Mohammad banned music in worship. In other settings Afghans often connect music with ungodly activities—with gatherings where there is drinking, gambling, and maybe even sexual activities like boy dancers who are used as sexual companions.

No well-bred family wants their son to grow up to be a fulltime musician, much less their daughter. Though musical skill may be appreciated, musicians themselves are considered marginal, according to a variety of research on Islam including *Music in the Mind: The Concepts of Music and Musician in Afghanistan*.[5] Some men may perform privately for family and friends. But a woman who sings in front of unrelated men? In traditional society she would be considered almost a prostitute. Otherwise, why would she put herself forward this way?

Christians can claim freedom in Christ, and their right to compose and perform. They can point to segments of Afghan society influenced by the modern world who access and create music publicly. But courtesy and appreciation for the Afghan traditional heritage may call us to exercise sensitivity.

Still, music is irrepressible. It flows out of the soul. To sing and play is human. Furthermore, in spite of its ambivalent status, Afghan music is the heir of complex classical traditions, some related to Persian music and others to Indian. At the simplest level, folk music and lullabies throb. And, in contrast to mainstream Sunni Muslims, the Sufis, Shiites, and Ismailis do sing hymns at religious events. These are not usually praise to God, but rather to religious heroes like Husain or the Aga Khan. Other beautiful, rhythmic sounds that wash over people's days are the call to prayer from the mosque and the chanting of the *Quran*. As for lyrics, it is said that all Afghans are poets. Certainly many can recite poetry for hours.

What a challenge for those who want to create worship songs to Jesus in Pashtu or Dari! It is true that radio, the internet, and global migration bombard people with all kinds of music. Still, enormous care—checking and rechecking the implications of performances—is appropriate for those who introduce worship music.

A simple project might experiment with a Pashtun poetic form called *landay*. This is only two lines long, the first line containing nine syllables and the second thirteen. Though short, these poems comment on relationships and events and give release to emotions. Some Pashtuns know hundreds of *landays*. Could Christian *landays* be created?

---

5 Sakata, *Music in the Mind.*

Going further, as more songs are composed, why not choose topics that add up to systematic teaching? In English-language worship services, unfortunately, many songs are so vague they could be directed to almost any deity. They lack particular gospel substance. But why not aim higher for a new set of Christian music? Why not cultivate a rich and balanced repertoire from the beginning? For example, by singing simple scriptural biographical ballads, Afghans could go through the hours of the day in the company of Moses and Hannah, Daniel and Esther, Paul and Lydia. Other songs could teach doctrines and Christian life practices, transmitting truth easily.

Of course such music must include themes that are important to Afghans. "Why do American Christians always sing happy songs?" Rashid wondered. Lament is a significant motif in the Bible. Hosea, Amos, and Habakkuk lament oppression, slavery, and injustice. Hannah laments barrenness. Job laments disease and loss. David and Jonah lament personal sin.

Who needs songs of lament more than Afghans? Refugees' sponsors encourage them to get busy, achieve goals and success, and be happy. If there were losses, let the wounds scab over quickly. But it takes time to heal. It takes time to honor who and what was lost. Afghans may need to stand inarticulately before the God who is eternal, who hears their lament in its incomprehensibility, who himself voluntarily entered into the suffering of the world. God is present for the wordless. In his time he will give words and music. Then some great Afghan Christian songs of lament may be born.

Celebrating

Life is hard. Babies die. Marauders invade. Crops fail. Stomachs shrink and still throb with hunger. Friends and relatives quarrel even when everything else is flourishing. Abysmal divisions crack the close connections that we depended on. That seems to be the way things are. We resign ourselves, and carry on.

Then suddenly a celebration erupts, and our understanding of reality flips: life is lavish, after all. We are awash in food, sports and games, so many friends and family, and more food. If the celebration is *Nawruz*, the red tulips are blooming. Pomegranates crunch between our teeth, and the juice runs down our chins.

Like the words of Scripture and the melodies of songs, the actions of celebrations may be avenues for worship. They declare that life is not just a rut of work and weariness. Some celebrations consecrate human connections, like weddings and even funerals. Some consecrate the mysterious but regular passing of time and the regularly changing landscape as it unfurls signs of springtime, then harvest, then winter. Some celebrations root us in history, as we remember leaders, courage, noble suffering, and heroic reawakenings.

All of them remind us that there is a rhythm to life. There will always be weddings. There will always be summer and winter. However bleak our circumstances, there will always be moments of renewal, and we exult in those. Those who follow Jesus bounce and skip with thanks to him for all his good gifts.

We celebrate with our bodies. Words and music touch our ears and voices, but celebratory actions involve all that we are, our entire physical selves. Using our hands and mouths, we cook and eat. Using our feet, we kick balls and dance. Into our chests we hug long-lost relatives and cuddle new babies. For ceremonies, we light candles, burn incense or daub perfume, and drape ourselves in gold jewelry and our surroundings in fine fabrics. All this honors God who made the material world and pronounced it good (Gen 1), who sanctified human bodies by inhabiting a body himself. Rituals and sacred dance and drama and even service activities all are ways that people use their bodies to worship God. For Afghans this is natural. When they were Muslim, they prayed not just with words but by standing shoulder to shoulder with others, then kneeling, and prostrating, and lifting hands to the sky.

Annual Religious Celebrations

Throughout the Muslim world there is a great holiday at the end of the fast of Ramadan. People slip into their finest clothes, gather and visit, and serve delicious foods. Women paint designs on their hands with henna. Beauty and gladness and savory tastes abound. This is one of the *Ids*, the sacred annual celebrations. The vast crowds, diversity of colors and fabrics and adornments, happy noise and hubbub, and tantalizing aromas and flavors underscore the importance of this event. They also showcase the joy of being alive. At such moments we are replenished. We are restocked to go forward into the hard months ahead, because we know that suffering is not everything. There will be more. Huge holidays give us hope.

Among Jesus's people, Christmas and Easter should be celebrated just as richly. They mark God's amazing acts. They connect us with brothers and sisters in countries and tribes all around the world—in cities and forests and mountains and deserts and islands—who mark these jubilees in their own unique ways. These holidays also foreshadow the greatest festivity of all. The book of Revelation in the Bible tells us there will be a party that will outshine all the parties that have ever been, all the *Ids* and *Nawruz* celebrations put together, all our most magnificent Christmas and Easter pageants. Zillions of people and creatures and forces will show up for that gala event. There will be dazzling jewels, light beyond electricity, a river of life, and a tree with leaves for the healing of the nations. Wars throughout the world will cease. God will wipe away all tears (Rev 20–21). What timely news for Afghans.

There is one more dimension of that cataclysmic finale: justice. There will be justice for those who have been wounded, oppressed, marginalized, raped, amputated, murdered, disenfranchised, evicted. Oppressors will be punished.

If joy is going to be real, there has to be justice. But that justice has a double edge. We ourselves have exploited others. We deserve punishment. Is there any way to escape the judgement of God's cosmic justice? Miraculously, yes. Those who throw themselves on the grace of the God, who himself took our punishment, those who are covered inexplicably by Christ's righteousness, they will be saved, and go free to enjoy the greatest party of all time—right in the middle of the Lamb's war, where we join a host extending through time and space to confront the powers of darkness. What an amazing, boggling, complex paradox.

Anticipating this ultimate party, our Christmas and Easter celebrations must be big. They must lavish sensory delights on those who attend, incorporating them into activities and social relationships. Discipleship is not just sequential Bible stories and their applications. Discipleship showers us with the exhilaration of being part of the whole great story. Annual celebrations bring the epic to life, and remind us who we are.

Besides Christian holidays, we honor others' special days. If an *Id* is coming—a major religious festival—we wish our friends a happy *Id*. If they invite us for a festive meal or event, we joyfully attend, and later reciprocate, maybe inviting them to a Christmas or Easter service as well as a meal. As noted in Chapters 6 and 8, some Muslim holidays offer conversational openers for sharing about Jesus: *Id al Adha* about the Lamb of God, and *Muharram* about the servant-leader who gives his life for the people.

The festival of spring, *Nawruz*, is one of the most important celebrations. Predating Islam, *Nawruz* affirms life. It exults in God's gift of regular rebirth, marked by the return of spring. During this holiday Afghans like to go out for picnics with traditional foods. In Los Angeles a few years ago, Christian Iranians joined twenty-five thousand other Iranians celebrating in a public park. There among the many food and craft stalls, Christians sold books and music packages in Farsi, a language also understood by many Afghans.

Life Cycle Celebrations

As well as annual celebrations, people everywhere mark important events in the personal life cycle. Births, puberty, weddings, and funerals are key transitions. Graduations, going to war or returning, going to sea or returning, creating a significant work of art, achieving an honor—all are events in a person's life that the community may honor. Some societies also have cleansing rituals. Women in the Old Testament underwent such rituals after giving birth. Navajos who have encountered violence or evil seek out a ceremony to restore their harmony with the rest of the cosmos. Christian women in Rwanda raped by soldiers have undergone a cleansing ritual to reaffirm their value.

Funerals deserve special attention. An Egyptian whose mother died while visiting America was shocked at how few people attended the funeral. She said, "My mother told me, 'You can skip a wedding, but never skip a funeral!'" A funeral is the culmination of a life, especially when it is for an older person. To attend that commemoration honors not just the person who died but all their family and friends. In some societies funerals are leisurely, lasting hours or even days. People reminisce about the person who has passed on. They savor stories. Some evangelists do most of their witnessing at funerals. They have found that these are excellent times to talk about meaning and eternity. People are receptive to big ideas at memorial events.

Births deserve attention, too. A baby is a miracle. The new person is an asset for the community (unless the people are starving). A ritual will mark this important arrival. Among Muslims, if the child is a boy, the ritual is circumcision. Just across the border from Afghanistan in the nation of Kazakhstan, circumcisions have become occasions for Christian witness. This developed spontaneously. Kazakh followers of Jesus naturally want their babies circumcised in a godly, spiritual context, as was the case when they were Muslims. So some of them include circumcisions in the regular church worship service. On that day, all their kin come to church, even though they are Muslim. They want to be present when this new person is honored and incorporated into their family. They hear the gospel, and afterwards share in a big feast.

All sorts of ordinary events can be sacramentalized through rituals. We pray for rain, and for a good planting or fishing season. Later we thank God for the harvest. Some people who move into a new house invite the whole church to come and pray for the house, blessing each room. Even our daily work can be blessed by rituals. One woman who is a writer places her hands on her computer and dedicates that day's output to the Lord before she writes a single word. Simple physical actions like these remind us that our ordinary lives have significance, and that God cares.

Beautiful words of Scripture and beautiful songs can be joined by beautiful acts of celebration to express worship, to teach, and to witness.

Praying

Women kneel silently on the carpet. Some rock back and forth. Others pray softly, fingering their beads as they count the repetitions of their recitations. Some speak audibly. Some sing quietly. Others echo the melody.

"I take refuge in You from the evil I have done, and I come to You in your grace to me, and I come to you in my sin, so forgive me, for there is no one who forgives sins except you," murmurs a woman. This is a Sufi Muslim prayer session called *dhikr*. Taking place in Syria, it represents beautiful worship in this tradition.[6]

Occasionally a woman will rise and sway, performing a simple, spontaneous liturgical dance, raising arms, shuffling feet, apparently impelled to offer her whole body as she reaches out to God. Here and there a few others stand up and sway, moved by their own rhythms. Then silence covers the worshippers again.

When they pray, the women beg God to be their refuge. They name the dangers that threaten them—uncertain health, or a job, or relationships, or politics, or spiritual forces and the evil eye. They praise God, and also the Prophet Muhammad, blessing him. They pray for Muslims throughout the world, for "our sisters" in places where there is conflict or oppression. At the end of the session, they recite the *Fatiha* together, the six verses of the first chapter of the *Quran*. As they conclude, some wipe their palms down over their faces, pulling the blessing of the recitation back onto themselves.

For Christians, prayer is one of our most basic activities. Our core focus is not the good acts that we do, nor even the right beliefs that we hold. No, our core focus is spending time with God. That is why we are Christians: to honor God, to know God, to "practice the presence of God," to "walk with God," to live in the reality that God is central to everything. Prayer is part of this. It includes confession, adoration, and asking, all circling around the God who is all power and all love.

Afghans are raised in prayer. Five times a day, a voice wafts through the air in their communities: "Come to prayer."

"No, I need to finish this," they might be tempted to respond, absorbed in whatever task they are tackling at that moment.

But the summons takes priority. "Your work will never be finished. There is always a new task. But God is here now, in the beginning and the middle and the end of all your days. Come to prayer."

This simple call nurtures an awareness of God in daily life. How they understand God may be skewed. God may be far off. God may be a stern taskmaster. God may not even speak their language. But God is there. Among Afghans, there are few atheists. Regular prayer nurtures this consciousness.

When Afghans come to Jesus, most of them do not continue with the five memorized daily prayers. Jesus has liberated them from legalism. However, Jesus's followers must continue to be prayerful people. What could be a greater privilege than talking with God all day long? Particularly when we can come boldly and directly to Him through the name of Jesus? "Let us then approach

---

6 Dale, "Dhikr: In the Heart."

God's throne of grace with confidence, so that we may receive mercy and find grace to help us in our time of need" (Heb 4:16).

As Afghan Christians learn to pray, they should follow neither a traditional Muslim pattern of prayer nor a Western Christian pattern. They should draw from the best in both hemispheres. Consider, for example, Sadhu Sundar Singh. He was an early twentieth century Indian Christian mystic who practiced the presence of God. Describing his prayer life, he said:

> As a diver holds his breath while he is diving, so a man of contemplation and prayer shuts himself in a chamber of silence, away from the distractions of the noisy world. Then he is able to pray with the Holy Spirit from above, without which it is impossible to lead a spiritual life ... To hear God's voice, we must wait for him in silence. Then, without voice or words, he will speak to the soul in the secret room of the heart ... The gift of ecstasy God has given me is far better than any home, and far greater than any hardship I might endure.[7]

Yet the Spirit always drew Sundar Singh back to serve the people. Disowned by his wealthy family, he wrapped himself in a yellow cloth, took up a walking stick, and wandered from place to place. Where people lingered, he would pause and talk about Jesus. He had a deep impact. Many believed. Lives changed. Sometimes he lived in a cave near a boys' school. Over time, the effect on these boys was profound. They began to serve low caste people and lepers, and when they graduated they chose careers of service.

None of us is Sundar Singh. His lifestyle is not ours. But he offers the model of a prayerful Asian Christian. Afghans must cultivate their own habits of prayer, individual and corporate. To avoid the dangers of heresy that threaten mystics, prayers must be rooted in Scripture. Then through prayer we will find our energy renewed. Through prayer we can offer a blessing to others. "May I pray for you?" is a question of tender concern. No matter how ignorant or weak we may be, through prayer we can connect people with the wisdom and wealth and power of God. What a high honor.

Sundar Singh emphasized getting away from noise. That is not always realistic. Yet even in the middle of chaos and pressure, prayer is possible. Hudson Taylor was the founder of the China Inland Mission. After years of spiritual struggle he discovered peace. When his friend Macartney asked how he could stay so serene amid enormous challenges, Taylor said, "My dear Macartney, the peace you speak of is in my case more than a delightful privilege, it is a necessity ... I could not possibly get through the work I have to do without the peace of God 'which passes all understanding' keeping my heart and mind."[8]

---

7 Comer, *Wisdom of the Sadhu*, 29, 40.

8 Edman, *They Found the Secret*, 20.

Taylor explained that he learned to draw nourishment from the Spirit of Jesus moment by moment, like a branch drawing sap from a vine (John 15).

Prayer ushers us into an alternate reality. This is what the women in the Sufi *dhikr* worship meetings were seeking—the privilege of being in the presence of God, lowly though we are. God is foundational to all our studying, singing, organizing, witnessing and serving. God is our priority. "We are called to an everlasting preoccupation with God, to be worshippers first and workers only second," said A. W. Tozer. "The work of a worshipper will have eternity in it."

Praying, storytelling, memorizing, singing, and celebrating animate our bodies and our hearts. Through these holistic activities, Afghans with venerable artistic traditions can enrich their worship. They can bathe in the beauty of Jesus, so glorious, so challenging, so powerful, so tender, the source of all that is lovely throughout all time and space.

— CHAPTER 10 —

Mountain Faith

Two stubborn questions and four stories of discipleship wrap up this book:

- *How does the modern secular world threaten Afghans' faith?*
- *How do we build healthy ethnic and multiethnic identities?*
- *Models of mature international discipleship*
- *A future for Afghans in the kingdom of God*

Is there hope for Afghanistan? Weapons have levelled homes and shops. Infrastructure has blown up. Terrorists run the government. Religious legalists squash the freedom of women. Tens of thousands of mothers die in childbirth. The economy is in the pits. International bankers refuse to invest. Opium seems to be the one sure thing that can bring in money and put food on the table.

An Afghan may be signing their death warrant if they call Jesus Lord.

Unquestionably the situation is tough. Loving Jesus as Lord in this land is like pushing a boulder up the Himalayas. Believers have died, and still more are going to die. Yet on a cosmic plane we know that death is followed by resurrection. Every day, and in every era, there is renewal and restoration through the Holy Spirit. This faith can move mountains. It is mountain faith.

Here in this final chapter we meet four Afghan Christians who are true internationals. They treasure their heritage but also interact across boundaries in the larger world. Their stories touch on two further issues: How can Afghan believers stand firm against the idols of the modern world? And how can migrants build healthy multiethnic identities?

Confronting Modern World Idols

Possibly the biggest challenge to discipleship is not religion or culture or biblical ignorance, but the seductions of the modern world. To grow into excellent disciples, Afghan believers must learn not only biblical basics, but also how to confront idols in the contemporary worldview.

"There are no atheists in foxholes," it is said. When deadly ammunition strafes overhead during a battle, the soldiers who take shelter in foxholes often can be heard praying. Even those who do not think about God in ordinary times suddenly call on his name when they are under fire. Similarly, the Afghans who were desperate to leave the country after the Taliban takeover in 2021 pled with God for help. Everyone took God seriously. There were no atheists then.

But things change when Afghans immigrate to a Western country, or even when conditions improve at home. God does not seem quite so important now. Instead, people are drawn to freedom and pleasure, money and things, and power and success. These are some of the idols of our time. They are extremely powerful attractions. In the end, they may be deadly to a sincere and godly faith.

Some migrants come to faith on their journey or after they reach their new land. But others give up the faith, especially teens and young adults. Now there are no bullets streaming overhead. There are no foxholes. Instead, there is so much else that dazzles and tempts—and frustrates and distracts and preoccupies. Who has time for God? Maybe as a security device on the side. A sort of good luck charm. But life with its pleasures and challenges and opportunities becomes an increasingly secular experience.

What a huge loss for Afghans who always have honored God, even before they knew Jesus as Lord. What a diminishment of their humanity. Once they worshipped with rich spirituality, even if it was misguided. Now they are lured to spend all their energies consuming and producing and seeking pleasure. This is a sadly reduced existence, however glamorous and exciting it may look from outside.

The idols of the modern world threaten believers as well as unbelievers. Tolerance and relativism are enormously popular, for example. Yet they may violate Jesus's unique supremacy. Even individualism may be dangerous. On the positive side, individualism offers freedom—free speech, free thought, free expression, free association. However, it can lead to lack of accountability and even to immorality. Afghans come from communal contexts, and this is a valuable part of their heritage.

How should individualism and community be balanced in the relations between generations or genders? Different believers will come to different conclusions in good faith. Overall, any potential idols in the contemporary worldview need to be pondered, named, illustrated, prayed over, and perhaps confronted. What is a good life? What is appropriate consumption? When should we say yes to material things? When should we say no? How should we structure our social relations so that they honor God? What principles should we follow as we wrestle with these decisions?

Planting seeds was the topic of a story that Jesus told (Luke 8). Afghans understand the cultivation of wheat seeds, vegetable seeds, and fruit tree seeds. Unfortunately, as Jesus pointed out, not all seeds bear fruit and produce a harvest. Various complications can stunt or kill the growth.

In Jesus's story, some seeds fall to the side of the path. They don't take root, and birds swoop down and gobble them up. Other seeds fall on dry, stony ground. They do take root and begin to grow, but then wither and die for lack of water. Other seeds have water but are surrounded by thorn bushes which shoot up and crowd out the new growth. Still, some seeds stretch roots down into good soil. Stems reach up into sunshine and rain, and these plants flourish and reproduce abundantly. In regard to this story, Jesus commented, "If anybody has ears, let him hear."

What a word for wise Afghan believers. Spiritual growth and maturity are not automatic. Dangers threaten from many sides. Some hazards drop on us when we least expect them. "If anybody has ears, let him hear."

Building Healthy Ethnic Identities

Who am I? Identity confuses a lot of people. One part of our identity is ethnic identity. For migrants that can pose a dilemma. Millions of Afghans have fled to Germany, Brazil, Canada, and elsewhere. Their children are growing up in new places. Are they Afghan? Canadian? Or what?

Even Afghans who do not migrate are flooded by global culture, especially through the media. All over the world people text from everywhere to everywhere. They match wits in the same video games and know the names of the same famous actors. Online they view the same material things—clothing, houses, recreational accoutrements—and crave these. They observe exciting new styles of social interaction. If they are fortunate, overseas kin will send money back home to invest in businesses, houses, education, and updated material things. Sometimes these global influences can weaken local Afghan values and social relationships.

Anthropologist Michael Rynkiewich describes the process:

> Globalization is the widespread engagement of people with an expanding worldwide system of communication, commerce, and culture that is

producing broad uniformities across selected sectors of many societies, as well as generating multiple hybrid cultures in various stages of reception, rejection, and reinvention.[1]

"Broad uniformities" across the world—maybe this slide is inevitable. Maybe cultural differences *should* diminish as the world gets "smaller." Does it matter?

Yes, it matters. Globalization is not enough. Specifically, it is not human enough. Anthropologist Rynkiewich adds, "Globalization commodifies everything." Social scientists recognize that human beings need roots in the rhythms of particular societies if they are going to flourish. We are nourished by the time-honored designs of friendship, courtship, marriage, parenting, aging, and dying. We are not just animals or robots or producers and consumers, we are persons born into communities with heritages. Being a global citizen ultimately makes an individual feel insignificant. But when you belong to a people, you have a place in time in the universe, a base for the conviction that you are part of the continuity of life flowing from the past and pulsing on into the future. You are in the story.

Afghan immigrant children may not speak Pashtu or Dari. They may pull away from their parents' traditions. When they grow up they may take jobs alongside other local citizens, shop in the same malls, go to the same sports events. They may even marry someone from another race. Are they still Afghan? Yes, they are still part of their people because they share a heritage. This includes:

- Descent from a particular ethnic community
- Common ancestral land (whether or not they ever travel there)
- Common ancestral language (whether or not they speak it)
- Common history, including stories of suffering and heroes
- Behaviors appropriate between close kin
- Holidays
- Humor

However, there are still more complications to ethnic identity. Clearly a person can have more than one. Think of an Afghan-American or Chinese-American or Arab-American. Sometimes one ethnic identity can "nest" inside another. For example, some Afghans speak Pashtu and others speak Dari. Both groups "nest" inside an overarching Afghan identity. All these identities are authentic.

---

1 Rynkiewich, *Soul, Self, and Society*, 234.

While affirming their own roots, believers must reach across gaps. They must make special efforts to love and affirm those in other ethnic groups. This may not be easy when there has been violence between the populations.

In sum, a cultural heritage matters. So does the modern world. Both dimensions are gifts from God. Yet either one can become toxic because both the cultural heritage and the modern world contain potential idols. In the words of Afghan-American Mariya Dostzadeh Goodbrake, migrants must "learn to navigate two cultures. Pick up what is beautiful in each and move forward, shedding what is bad."[2] This is the route to carving and polishing healthy multiethnic identities.

Here are four Afghan followers of Jesus who are learning to do that.

Honest Leaders

Every morning Haleem stepped out of his family courtyard and searched for some van to transport him through the dust and bougainvillea to the center of Kabul. Bumping around potholes and swerving through exhaust fumes, they eventually reached their destination. Haleem would get out and stride through the high gate of his office building. There he would spend the day processing financial figures.

His solid education was a blessing. It had paved the way for a pretty good life. Still, Haleem was ambitious, always on the lookout for improvements. One day he heard some acquaintances talking about a study program in which they were enrolled.

"Excuse me. I overheard something about a course you are taking. May I ask what kind of course it is?" he asked.

"Leadership," they answered. "It's a twenty-six-week course on leadership. The lecturers include internationals from several different countries. Their ideas really make you think."

Haleem lost no time in discovering where the classes were located. Soon he himself was enrolled. As his friends had reported, the teachers did make him think in new ways. Students were encouraged to explore: What are your core values? What do you desire for yourself? What do you desire for your community? It was unusual to think so freely and reflect so honestly. Undergirding good leadership is integrity, the students were taught. Making money is not enough. There must be honesty and trust. This will result in hope. The teachers themselves seemed to radiate a transformed kind of existence.

"There's something so good here, it's like a magnet," Haleem murmured to himself.

---

2 Mariya Dostzadeh Goodbrake, interview with Miriam Adeney, Feb. 25, 2023.

For the internship component of the program, Haleem was sent to Kazakhstan. Here he encountered Kazakhs who lived with the same kind of integrity. Even Kazakhs!

One day the program's leader revealed to Haleem that he was a follower of Jesus. He shared what he read in the Holy Book, and how he prayed. Haleem discovered other believers among the instructors, as well as among those in Kazakhstan. Over time he learned more about Scripture and about Christian community. "Eventually I could no longer resist the invitation to be in God's family," he says.

He told his wife Hafiza. Many a wife would be upset and would complain to her father, or to his. Divorce might be the result, or even death. But Hafiza kept quiet about Haleem's change, because he consistently honored her and treated her well. They had three daughters. A lot of men would have been disappointed. So many girls one after another, and never a son! But Haleem would point to his wife and daughters and smile and say, "These are my four angels."

Like Haleem, Hafiza was educated. She worked as a schoolteacher. When he told her what had happened to him and announced his new commitments, she merely said, "I will have to consider this."

While she has been considering, God has blessed them with a son!

Celebrating Easter Is Not Enough

Mohammad Ali was a boy in northern Afghanistan when his people were massacred. Thousands were butchered. He was ambling home from a field when he heard motors revving and then shots and screams. He slunk behind boulders and hid. Finally, though the screams continued, it seemed the shots had stopped. Mohammad stepped out and made his way cautiously to his own family compound.[3]

Along the way he saw bodies—so many bodies that he could hardly avoid stepping on them.

Up to now, life had been good in this simple town of mud houses with cows and goats and chickens roaming around. Mohammad and his friends flew kites and challenged each other with riddles. In the evenings they ran to a nearby farm and brought back newly-picked melons. On their rooftop patio they enjoyed the fruit with fresh naan and milk and sugar.

But now life was no longer safe. The men of the family—who would be killed immediately if they were found—hid out in the fields. The women hovered at home, but soldiers came and ordered them to remove their *burqas* and gang raped Mohammad's prettiest cousin. Although he was just a young boy, Mohammad took over running the family store.

---

3 Ali, *Journey of Transformation*.

Of course, that was not safe either. Who knew when the gunmen might return and blast anyone who was left? Eventually, joining with other boys, Mohammad fled into the hills. He was at a disadvantage in this scramble, however. An accident some years earlier had cost him one leg. On level ground, he navigated pretty nimbly, using a crutch. Climbing rough mountains was another matter.

He kept up as best he could. Their life was bleak. With no food, they ate weeds and even dirt. Illness and fevers plagued them.

One day, although Mohammad was very sick, the boys forced him to get up and go to a stream to wash before prayers. If he did not join them in their ritual prayers, he might bring a curse down on the group, they feared. Groggily Mohammad hobbled and stumbled toward the brook. But on a slope he slipped and fell. Down the rough, stony hillside he crashed, with his crutch clanging along behind. His head hit a rock. He landed beside a ditch. He could not move. Darkness enveloped him and he felt that he was going to die.

Then he cried out to Jesus. Up to now he had been calling on all the prophets, one after another. Now he begged, "Jesus, I am crying. I am praying to you. I know you are one of the important prophets. Please heal me."

Shortly after that he was able to get up and walk as usual. That night he slept well, and the next day he felt healthy. From that point on, he determined to know more about Jesus.

Moving into a slightly more urban environment, the boys collected scrap metal to sell so that they could buy food. One afternoon, as Mohammad was carrying his collected metal to the buyer, he spied a wind-up radio. Instead of buying food, he bought the radio.

No signal was available in the valley, so Mohammad hiked up the mountain until a radio signal came through. What he heard was a Bible story, the story of Samson. This prophet had suffered but had given his life to save his people. Over time Mohammad heard several Old Testament stories. Eventually he would discover that these accounts were connected to the story of Jesus, the very person he was desperate to hear about.

His appetite was whetted. "I want to meet a person who knows about Jesus," he decided. Not just stories floating on the air waves, but a real person.

A United Nations team came to the town center to distribute food. Mohammad heard that there were Americans on the team. He had also heard that Americans knew about Jesus. He showed up at the food distribution, and watched the Americans, but was too intimidated to push himself forward with his question.

In time Mohammad would make his way by foot across Afghanistan, Iran, and Turkey. There he would encounter Iranian believers and would meet

Jesus personally. Today he is a strong Christian. Although he no longer lives in Afghanistan, he coordinates and helps fund programs inside the country that serve basic needs, especially schooling for children and income-generating projects for women. Through the internet he also trains and encourages witnesses and Christian leaders.

In March 2023, on the first day of Ramadan, Mohammad wrote,

> All of us followers of Christ are gearing up and getting ready for Easter. But there is another holiday that started today. Roughly two billion people began celebrating Ramadan, Islam's holiest month.
>
> For an entire month Muslims around the world will fast from dawn to dusk. No food. No water. This is a massive global event for Muslims in which they also pray and give to charity.
>
> This should also be significant for Christians. On Easter we will celebrate Christ's victory over death, and his glorious resurrection. Ramadan is a reminder that there are billions of people who do not believe or have not even heard this good news, and millions of those people are Afghanis. [Let us] join in prayer for our Muslim neighbors, that their hearts would be open to the true God and King of all the universe.[4]

Here we see Mohammad's heart for his people. Comfortably celebrating Easter is not enough when millions know nothing except Ramadan.

The Woman Who Loves Soccer

The day that Mariya's father met her pastor was a watershed moment. It was a turning point in a long journey. Back in Afghanistan, Mariya's family owned extensive lands. When the Russians invaded, her grandfather immediately got all his sons out of the country. Their families followed and reunited in Iran. For the next five years they eked out a living in that country. Mariya's dad had been in the Ministry of Transportation and her mom had been a schoolteacher, but now in Iran her dad sold T-shirts on the street. The Iranians merely tolerated them, and eventually offered to pay for their plane tickets if they would go back to Afghanistan.

Mariya's family boarded the plane, but got off in India, where they spent the next five years. Eventually friends and relatives in India moved on to Europe. Preparing to do the same, Mariya's father sold everything and borrowed the rest of his inheritance from his father, who sent it from Afghanistan.

A cousin came to visit and stole all the money.

Desperate, they were advised to go to the Canadian embassy. A kindly official approved their papers joking, "The first thing you must do is pick up snow and rub it on your daughters' cheeks!" When they landed in Canada they

---

4 Mohammad Ali, personal newsletter, March 2023.

were grateful but also scared, because they were the only ones in all their kin group to come to North America.

Still, at last they were settled. As time passed and they felt more at home, Mariya began to develop a sort of split identity. She figured out how to be Muslim Afghan with her family but Western with others. In general Canadian society, she reveled in the freedom, broadmindedness, expanded worldview, and resilience. At the same time, she loved the Afghan values of hospitality, etiquette, loyalty, and the food and the language in her home, where her parents tried to preserve a little oasis of Afghanistan.

These identities collided for Mariya on September 11, 2001, when terrorist-piloted jets crashed into the World Trade Center towers. As part of the first non-White family in their neighborhood, Mariya had found it easier to introduce herself as Persian. But when students and teachers crowded around TVs and said negative things about Afghans, she reclaimed her identity. She stepped up on a chair and shouted, "I'm Muslim. I'm from Afghanistan. So what?"

However, her disillusionment was profound when her dad whisked her beloved but somewhat wild 16-year-old sister back to Afghanistan. There he married his daughter off to her cousin. "This is the act of a vicious dad," Mariya thought. Only years later did she come to empathize with him, to see that he had been stripped of everything, and the only thing he had left was his reputation.

Graduation at last! Mariya was gifted with a one-week vacation to Mexico, to be followed by some time in New York. For some reason, she deliberately overslept and missed her flight from Mexico back to the US. She stayed on in Playa del Carmen, a Mexican mecca for hippies and New Agers. While there, along with her friends, she experimented with Mayan religion, worshipping the full moon. Up to that point she had never thought much about relating personally to God. Allah was too high. She could not picture approaching him. But the moon goddess might be accessible.

Meanwhile she kept running into John Smith, a man whose family had a health center in a Mayan village. This was a base for rotating teams of US surgeons who came every month. Mariya began to volunteer and soon was the administrative lead, coordinating the teams. She did this for the next three years. Her parents hated the fact that she was living away from her family in a foreign country, and even more that she was working in a Christian clinic. To save face, they told their friends, "She's doing some studies in Mexico."

The story of Jesus, the personal prayers, and most of all the beautiful interaction between John and his wife and children touched Mariya. Even though some things seemed weird, the gospel drew her. She worried over it. "I would have to stop being Afghan if I wanted to become a follower of Jesus," she thought. Still, she began to follow.

Several years later, she found herself part of a church in Kansas City. She was still troubled with a sense of split identity, half Muslim Afghan and half Western Christian. The pastor told her, "Mariya, you need to understand who you were as a Muslim. You need to build a bridge back."

As she took time to do that, she saw that the gospel is not a foreign message for Afghans. "Christ was always there. Now I see his fingerprints. He grew up in the Middle East. He is more connected to our heritage than to the West. I just had a veil over my eyes, and couldn't see him." Now she says, "God put me in an Afghan home. I can hold onto the beautiful things in my culture, while abandoning the things that don't glorify God. I am Afghan. No one can take that away from me."

The meeting between Mariya's father and her pastor was a watershed moment. This happened when Mariya was getting married.

In Afghanistan, women go from their father's home to their husband's home. For years her father had worried about her being alone in North America, and desperately wanted her to get married. What a relief he felt when she told him she was engaged. That was the good news. The bad news (for him) was that her fiancé was a Christian.

It took about four months of negotiations, using her sisters as intermediaries, until finally her father agreed to come to the wedding in Kansas City. The whole family drove all night, traveling south from Toronto. They walked stiffly into the pastor's house for the rehearsal dinner, dressed to the nines, entering in order of status. They sat down politely but tensely.

Then the pastor said to her father, "We come from different religions, different countries, different cultures. But we have the same story. We are both men who have found ourselves in the middle of a war. (The pastor had been in El Salvador, and when the violence broke out he had not left but had stayed and served as a mediator.) And we have both brought our daughters to this place of hope and safety."

Mariya's father and her family began to thaw. Out of their disparate stories, the pastor had created a third story. He had tapped into their common humanness and shared experiences.

When her family left that night, before her father got into the car, Mariya asked him, "How was it? How did you feel about the evening?"

"I'm confused," he said.

"Why?"

"Well, those Christians are just like Muslims," he answered. He had lived in North America for fifteen years, but this was the first time he had had a meal in a Western home and experienced genuine hospitality.

Awareness of that gap propels Mariya's work now. She has founded Global FC, an agency that serves refugees. When she first moved to Kansas City, she enjoyed the diversity that she saw in the local refugee community, and got acquainted with some of the people. Then she went on a church mission trip to a huge refugee camp in Jordan. In that camp she saw that children could be sparks of hope. Back home she prayed: "God, give me a tool to bless our refugees here."

God answered: "Soccer."

In refugee camps, children play soccer, but when they are resettled they often do not have access to clubs or leagues or transportation. Mariya changed that. Global FC (Football Community) enrolls three hundred refugee children in top-tier soccer competition. More than that, they "build a village around a kid. Instead of one person supporting that kid, our three departments offer education and mentoring that is mandatory." Twelve to fifteen caring adults are available to interact with each child.

Through the children, the team gets acquainted with the families. "It is vital for our success to have a high level of engagement with the family," Mariya says. "Although we're living in an individualistic society, we want long-term sustainable impact with these communally-oriented people."

In the beginning, Mariya asked a local NGO, "Hey, give me twelve kids!" The first twelve were from nine countries. She tackled the two biggest barriers: transportation and costs. She found a good coach and aimed for excellence, with high competitive opportunities and even Olympic connections.

Her work became visible in the community. Sporting Kansas City chose her for the MVP award. The *Kansas City Star* posted an in-depth story on Global FC on Thanksgiving, the biggest viewing day of the year. In 2020 Mariya won the grand prize for her short film *Long Road to Freedom* in the Women's Film Festival sponsored by Empower Women Media.

Meanwhile, the work goes on. Global FC's mentoring varies, depending on various children's needs. For example, some mentors do career counseling, while others offer one-to-one personal interaction. "A great team of volunteers" makes the difference, Mariya says. As they spend time with families, they do encounter issues beyond their expertise, like a home eviction or a complicated pregnancy. "We can't do it all. But we network with an ecosystem of community resource partners. We can call on them. There is a high collaborative spirit."

Crime and violence are reduced when such sports programs are in place. Citing a parallel set of uprooted people, Mariya observes: "Rwanda used soccer to turn child soldiers back into children."

In her Christian witness Mariya proceeds slowly. She believes in the power of story—her pastor's story, her father's story, the refugee kids' stories. Ultimately these pave the way to share the greatest story of all, she says. Timing and credibility matter. People watch and wonder: "There is something that is influencing those Christians to be like that. What is it?" That may be the moment to give them a Bible in their language.

"God is bringing the nations to our door," Mariya says. Whether the ministry is physical or spiritual, "it is pure disobedience not to reach out to refugees."

Teaching That Is Deep and Wide

"Whoever wants to be dedicated to Holy War, step forward!" The year was 2001. For three hours the speaker bombarded Luke's school class with glorious rhetoric about Osama bin Laden.[5]

Luke took God seriously and prayed regularly. So he stepped forward. He received enthusiastic congratulations, and a black turban.

But when his father saw the turban, he exploded. "There will be no life of violence for you. Go back and get your name off that list at once."

Providentially the school principal, a family friend, had not added Luke's name to the list.

Luke was the rare boy who graduated from high school in his province. Making his way to Kabul, he enrolled in medical school and eventually became an x-ray technician. In religion classes he asked questions: "God spoke to Moses. Why doesn't he speak to me?" His teachers told him to be quiet. Eventually he decided to quit focusing on religion. But he did not quit thinking about God. Anatomy and physiology classes would not let him forget the incredible designs programmed into the universe by a Creator.

Some Korean friends prayed. He assumed they were Buddhist, but they said, "No, we're Christian." He asked them for a Bible. They were too scared to give him one, but said, "Just come to our Friday night studies." There he read the Bible. John 10:10 spoke to him powerfully: "The thief comes only to steal and kill and destroy; I have come that they may have life, and have it to the full."

After two years, Luke believed.

Then he married Sarah. They were engaged before they were born! Their fathers had agreed that if the babies were a boy and a girl, they would marry. Luke told Sarah about his new faith. She had no idea what it meant, but agreed to stick with him. In time she too believed. "I came from a dark place into the light," she says.

They had Christian friends from Korea, the US, Bangladesh, and Egypt who were living and working in Afghanistan. Nurtured by these friends, Luke stepped out and talked with many Afghans about Jesus. He encouraged brothers and sisters to form worship groups. Around the country hundreds of new Christians were being born into faith.

---

5 Zylstra, "Escape from Kabul."

Then fifty officers raided Luke's home. He was handcuffed to the bed, and Sarah was held at gunpoint. When their child cried, a policewoman advised Sarah to plead ignorance. She did, and was released. Luke was imprisoned for a month on the charge of provoking differences between religions. Providentially, before the police could download the information in his laptop containing names and addresses of other Christians, the laptop was stolen.

Other prisoners beat Luke. Killing him would be a righteous act, they argued. Only ethnic rivalries in the jail kept him alive. Guards beat Luke too. Eventually he signed a confession that he had converted to faith in the Lord Jesus Christ. This meant death. Now, however he felt release and peace and freedom to share his faith with all the other prisoners while he waited to be executed.

Luke's family did not know about his faith until they saw his arrest on TV. His family blamed Sarah. Her family, of course, blamed Luke and wanted a divorce. The neighbors wanted to take their children away from both of them.

Unexpectedly, Luke was freed. Sarah's family locked her in a room so she could not see him. But she escaped, came to him, and told him she would go wherever he wanted.

They quickly left the country. After several months, they returned. Afghanistan was home, and it was where they were called to serve. Luke took construction jobs, and the rest of the time he witnessed, discipled, and networked with other Christian leaders. He saw groups multiply, and cheered them on. The Afghan house church network was emerging. Over the next four years, Luke and Sarah would move eleven times. They always had a suitcase packed and some food ready to carry along. If Sarah had two days' notice, she could pack up the entire house, storing all the household goods in boxes.

Danger escalated. Some Christians were killed. Luke was a wanted man. It was time to move to the United Arab Emirates. There they met two American pastors in an international church who invited Luke to become an intern. With them, he studied biblical and systematic theology. He learned that preaching must be built from a text, not a topic. He saw how the whole Bible is a unity, with the Old Testament stories pointing to Christ. Now he was preparing for ministry that would be deep as well as wide.

Meanwhile, from afar he kept nurturing dozens of Christian leaders in Afghanistan. To share what he was learning, he invited two of them to meet him in India. There he taught them how to exegete and exposit Ephesians. Later he invited Afghan pastors to travel to the UAE for modular courses on Bible and theology. Some heavy textbooks were translated into Afghan languages. Luke created a YouVersion Bible reading plan for Afghans, a website, and a podcast where seekers could ask questions.

By 2021, there were an estimated ten thousand Christians in Afghanistan. That year 120 of them took a daring new step: they legally changed their ID cards' religious status from Muslim to Christian.

But later that year the Taliban took over. Suddenly Christians were in peril.

"Run!" Luke advised the pastors and leaders, because the Taliban tended to shoot first and ask questions later. "Fly out, or drive out. Get rid of your Bibles. Delete the data on your laptops. Destroy your flash drives." One pastor couldn't bear to burn his theology books, so he put them on the street, hoping people would steal and read them.

Sixty Christian families were in hiding for several weeks, homeless, camping, some with babies. Christians in the UAE tracked the believers in Afghanistan daily and arranged for safe houses. They bought *burqa* coverings for the women and sent in extra cash. Eventually the UAE friends helped hundreds of believers exit to Iran, the UAE, Brazil, Tajikistan, the US, or other places.

Believers continue in Afghanistan, however, and new followers of Jesus have joined them. Luke's social media platform is "lighting up with messages, hundreds of them, from people in Afghanistan with spiritual questions: Where is God? Does God exist? Is he good or not?"[6] Some of those who are contacting him are people Luke has known for years, but many are strangers. "We send them the link to read the Bible," he says.

Mountain Faith

Even when mountains are invisible, even when they are hidden behind clouds and fog, they never go away. Although we cannot see them, we know that they are there, poking up into the sky. If we live among mountains, we are absolutely sure that they will reappear to loom over and amaze and awe us. Yet no matter how familiar, sometimes they catch us unaware. Then for an instant we pull up short, breathless in the face of grandeur and majesty.

Mountains lift us out of our humdrum selves to a higher realm. The Psalmist sang, "I will lift up my eyes to the hills" (Psalm 121). Pacific Northwest author Timothy Egan, thinking about the mountains where he loves to hike, wrote, "In the last light of day we can look up, from the low point of urban stress, and see the high point of outdoor relief—the natural neon of alpenglow."[7] When Everest mountaineer Willie Unsoeld was asked, "Why do people climb mountains?" he reportedly answered, "Because the top of a mountain is the only place where we can find convergence. It is the only place where all the lines come together."

---

6 Zylstra, "Escape."

7 Egan, *Good Rain*, 8.

Afghanistan has six hundred miles of major mountains. Alongside the rugged landscape, Afghanistan has rugged people. This book showcases stories of Afghans who are following Jesus, like Haleem, Mohammad Ali, Mariya, and Luke. Many dimensions of their life and faith have been explored. How do these believers find community? What gospel bridges tap into an Afghan Muslim worldview? How do storytelling, memorization, music, celebrations, and prayer strengthen disciples? How are small businesses developed? What is an ideal Afghan woman? What are challenges of Christian marriage for Afghans, and how can these be tackled? How about Christian child raising? How can refugees and immigrants build healthy ethnic identities?

Beyond the mountains of Afghanistan there are valleys with wheat, vegetables, fruits, sheep, goats, camels, and cattle. In the ground are abundant resources, from lapis lazuli to lithium. In villages there are looms with shimmering carpets. There are community associations that provide order, solve problems, and plan new directions. On the larger cultural scene, there are infusions from Persia in the west, India and Pakistan in the east, the "stans" to the north, and from larger Western and Eastern blocs.

In history, there have been wise national leaders like Ahmad Shah Durrani. As for Christian believers, they have been here almost since the time of Pentecost—even if very few—constituting continuing threads in the carpet of Christ's followers. Today there are Afghans who call Jesus Lord in thirty countries. Worldwide there are nearly forty million Afghans. All of them are created in the image of God, offered new life through Jesus's death, and fashioned for active service in God's world.

Some of the people described in this book have wrestled with unspeakable hardships. Through it all, they have continued to look up, longing for convergence and coherence, yearning for something more. In the spirit of the archetypical shepherd—tough, competent, natural, responsible, and free— some have come to honor and worship the great Shepherd who gave his life for his sheep. Their faith soars above the mountains in praise to their Creator and Savior, an enduring, strong resource that will bless the future of Afghanistan.

These faithful stewards prepare for the day when they can join the crowds around God's throne to sing praise in Pashtu and Dari and every other Afghan language. In the meantime, Afghan followers of Jesus aim to serve people right now wherever they find themselves, as God empowers and fills them to be channels of his love.

Bibliography

Abdo, Genevieve, and Dulia Mogahed. "What Muslim Women Want." *Wall Street Journal*, December 13, 2006.

Adeney, Miriam. "Conclusion: A Place Called Home." In *Refugee Diaspora: Missions amid the Greatest Humanitarian Crisis of the World*, edited by Sam George and Miriam Adeney, 167–74. Littleton, CO: William Carey Publishing, 2018.

Adeney, Miriam. *Kingdom Without Borders: The Untold Story of Global Christianity.* Downers Grove, IL: InterVarsity Press, 2009.

Ahmed, A. S. *Mataloona: Pukho Proverbs*. Karachi, Pakistan: Oxford University Press, 1975.

Ahmed, A. S. *Pukhtun Economy and Society: Traditional Structure and Development in a Tribal Society*. London: Routledge and Kegan Paul, 1980.

Ahmed, A. S. *Social and Economic Change in the Tribal Areas*. Karachi, Pakistan: Oxford University Press, 1977.

Ali, Mohammad. *A Journey of Transformation from the Heart of Afghanistan*. N.p.: Illumify Media Global, 2021.

Anderson, J. W. "How Afghans Define Themselves in Relation to Islam." In *Revolutions and Rebellions in Afghanistan: Anthropological Perspective*, edited by M. N. Shahrani and R. L. Canfield, 281. Bloomington: Indiana University Press, 2022.

Asia Foundation. *A Survey of the Afghan People*. N.p.: The Asia Foundation, 2017.

Azoy, Whitney. "Reputation, Violence, and *Buzkashi*." In *Local Politics in Afghanistan: A Century of Intervention in the Social Order*, edited by Conrad Schetter, 97–110. New York: Colombia University Press, 2013.

Barfield, Thomas. *Afghanistan: A Cultural and Political History*. Princeton, NJ: Princeton University Press, 2010.

Comer, Kim. *Wisdom of the Sadhu: Teaching of Sundar Singh*. Walden, NY: Plough Publishing House, 2000.

Cragg, Kenneth. *The House of Islam*. Encino, CA: Dickenson Publishing Co., 1975.

Cramer, Christopher, and Jonathan Goodhand. "Try Again, Fail Again, Fail Better? War, the State, and the 'Post–Conflict' Challenge in Afghanistan," *Development and Change* 33, no. 5 (2002): 885–909.

Dale, Moira. "Dhikr: In the Heart of Faith," *When Women Speak* (blog), February 11, 2018. https://whenwomenspeak.net/blog/dhikr-in-the-heart-of-faith/.

DeLange, Angela. "Discipling Iranian Children in North America." Unpublished Paper, 2020.

Denny, Frederick Mathewson. *Introduction to Islam*. New York: Macmillan Publishing Co., 1985.

Dupre, Louis. *Afghanistan*. Princeton, NJ: Princeton University Press, 1973.

Easton, David. *A Systems Analysis of Political Life*. New York: Wiley, 1965.

Edman, V. Raymond. *They Found the Secret: Twenty Transformed Lives*. Grand Rapids, MI: Zondervan, 1960.

Egan, Timothy. *The Good Rain: Across Time and Terrain in the Pacific Northwest*. New York: Random House Vintage Books, 1990.

Elphinstone, Mountstuart. "An Account of the Kingdom of Caubul, and its Dependencies, in Persia, Tartary, and India (1842) - Volume I." *Books in English*, 14. https://digitalcommons.unomaha.edu/afghanuno/14/.

Garrison, David. "The Western South Asia Boom." In *A Wind in the House of Islam*. Monument, CO: WIGtake Resources, 2014.

Gonzalez, Justo. *Manana: Christian Theology from a Hispanic Perspective*. Nashville, TN: Abingdon Press, 1990.

Hechter, Michael. *Containing Nationalism*. New York: Oxford University Press, 2000.

Ingram, Edward. "Great Britain's Great Game: An Introduction," *International History Review* 11, no. 1 (1980): 160–71.

Jafar, Husain Mufti Sahib. *Qibla Nahjul Balagha*. Karachi, Pakistan: Bookhome, 1971.

Karim, Ahmad. "Three Times a Refugee: Journey of an Afghani Doctor." In *Refugee Diaspora: Missions amid the Greatest Humanitarian Crisis of the World*, edited by Sam George and Miriam Adeney, 11–17. Littleton, CO: William Carey Publishing, 2018.

King, Martin Luther. *Baccalaureate Address*. Wesleyan University, 1964.

Lausanne Movement for World Evangelization. "There Are No Unreached Children" (advance paper, Lausanne Movement for World Evangelization, Cape Town, 2010). https://lausanne.org/content/there-are-no-unreached-children#:~:text=There%20are%20no%20'unreached'%20children,to%20know%20and%20follow%20Jesus.

Lehr, Rachel. "Mending Afghanistan Stitch by Stitch: How Traditional Crafts and Social Organization Advance Afghan Women." In *Land of the Unconquerable: The Lives of Contemporary Afghan Women*, edited by Jennifer Heath and Ashraf Zahedi. Berkeley: University of California Press, 2011.

Lindholm, C. *Generosity and Jealousy: The Swat Pukhtuns of Northern Pakistan*. New York: Columbia University Press, 1982.

Lipset, Seymour Martin. "Some Social Requisites of Democracy: Economic Development and Political Legitimacy." *American Political Science Review* 53, no. 1 (1959): 169–205.

Makarian, Krikor. "Today's Iranian Revolution: How the Mullahs Are Leading the Nation to Jesus." *Mission Frontiers* 30, no. 5 (2008): 6–13.

Migdal, Joel. *Strong Societies and Weak States: State-Society Relations and State Capabilities in the Third World*. Princeton, NJ: Princeton University Press, 1988.

Monsutti, Alessandro. "Trust, Friendship and Transversal Ties Among Afghans." In *Local Politics in Afghanistan: A Century of Intervention in the Social Order*, edited by Conrad Schetter, 147–62. New York: Colombia University Press, 2013.

"A New Drug War," *Economist* (2023): 28.

Open Doors. "Afghanistan." *The 2022 World Watch List*.

Passarlay, Gulwali, and Nadene Ghouri. *The Lightening Sky*. New York: HarperOne, 2016.

Prior, Karen Swallow. *Fierce Convictions: The Extraordinary Life of Hannah More, Poet, Reformer, Abolitionist*. Nashville, TN: Nelson Books, 2014.

Putnam, Robert D. *Making Democracy Work: Civic Traditions in Modern Italy*. Princeton, NJ: Princeton University Press, 1993.

Rashid, Ahmed. "Sister Courage: Hazara Women Take to the Battlefield." *Far East Economic Review* (Nov. 27, 1997): 30.

Reilly, Benjamin. *Democracy in Divided Societies: Electoral Engineering for Conflict Management*. Cambridge: Cambridge University Press, 2001.

Rutledge, Fleming. *The Crucifixion: Understanding the Death of Jesus Christ*. Grand Rapids, MI: Eerdmans, 2015.

Rynkiewich, Michael. *Soul, Self, and Society: A Postmodern Anthropology for Mission in a Postcolonial World*. Eugene, OR: Cascade Books, 2011.

Sakata, Hiromi Lorraine. *Music in the Mind: The Concepts of Music and Musician in Afghanistan*. Kent, OH: Kent State University Press, 1983.

Scott, Karen. "The Influence of Community Development and Micro-Credit Programs on the Status and Role of Rural Bangladeshi Muslim Women: A Paradigm for Discipleship." PhD diss., Fuller Theological Seminary, 2007.

Simpson, St. John. *Afghanistan: A Cultural History*. Northampton, MA: Interlink Books, 2012.

Smith, Deborah. "Between Choice and Force: Marriage Practices in Afghanistan." In *Land of the Unconquerable: The Lives of Contemporary Afghan Women*, edited by Jennifer Heath and Ashraf Zahedi. Berkeley: University of California Press.

Spain, J. W. *The Way of the Pathans*. Karachi, Pakistan: Oxford University Press, 1972.

Stasavage, David. *The Decline and Rise of Democracy: A Global History from Antiquity to Today*. Princeton, NJ: Princeton University Press, 2020.

Steinbeck, John. *The Grapes of Wrath*. New York: Penguin Books, 2002.

Stockdale, A. A. "God Left the Challenge in the Earth." *His* (December 1964): 20.

Tolkien, J. R. R. "On Fairy Stories." In *Essays Presented to Charles Williams*, edited by C. S. Lewis, 33–89. Oxford: Oxford University Press, 1947.

Tucker, Ruth, and Walter Liefeld. *Daughters of the Church*. Grand Rapids, MI: Zondervan, 1987.

USAID. "USAID/Afghanistan Education Fact Sheet." April 15, 2023. https://www.usaid.gov/afghanistan/our-work/education.

Von Kaehne, Peter. "Iranian Diaspora Ministry." In *Scattered and Gathered: A Global Compendium of Diaspora Missiology*, edited by Sadiri Joy Tira and Tetsunao Yamamori, 445–46. Cornwall, UK: Regnum Books, 2016.

WHO. "World Health Organization/Afghanistan." April 1, 2023. https://www.emro.who.int/afg/programmes/health-system-strengthening.html.

Wilbur, Donald. *Afghanistan: People, Society, Culture*. New Haven, CT: HRAF Press, 1962.

Wilson, J. Christy. *Afghanistan: The Forbidden Harvest*. Elgin, IL: David C. Cook Publishing Co., 1981.

Yunus, Muhammad. "The MicroLoan." *Seattle Post-Intelligencer* (Sept. 29, 1996): E1–3.

Zucchino, David. "Female Judges in Afghanistan Now Jobless and in Hiding." *Seattle Times* (October 21, 2021).

Zylstra, Sarah Eikoff. "Escape from Kabul." *The Gospel Coalition Podcast*, April 29, 2022. https://www.thegospelcoalition.org/podcasts/recorded/escape-from-kabul.

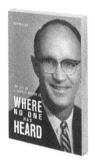

Where No One Has Heard: The Life of J. Christy Wilson Jr.

Ken Wilson | Paperback & ePub

Read the first full biography of the humble, adventurous man of prayer who helped launch the Urbana missions conference, pioneered ministry in Afghanistan when others thought it impossible, mobilized hundreds of students toward world evangelization, and reintroduced the biblical idea of leveraging one's profession for the kingdom with the term "tentmaking." Riveting, uplifting, and frequently amusing, this book will challenge you to reconsider what is possible when we dare to yield to Christ and his purposes in the world.

Refugee Diaspora: Missions amid the Greatest Humanitarian Crisis of the World

Miriam Adeney and Sam George, Editors | Paperback & ePub

Refugee Diaspora is a contemporary account of the global refugee situation and how the light of the gospel of Jesus Christ is shining brightly in the darkest corners of the greatest crisis on our planet. These hope-filled pages of refugees encountering Jesus Christ presents models of Christian ministry from the front lines of the refugee crisis and the real challenges of ministering to today's refugees. It includes biblical, theological, and practical reflections on mission in diverse diaspora contexts from leading scholars as well as practitioners in all major regions of the world.

Facing Fear: The Journey to Mature Courage in Risk and Persecution

Anna Hampton | Paperback & ePub

Facing Fear is a practical guide for believers who long to have bold, mature courage. Cultivating this courage is necessary to endure wisely for Christ's sake. Anna Hampton integrates exegesis and psychology to explain how humans respond to fear and how the Holy Spirit enables us to make a different choice than our normal. Learning to face our fears, name them, and manage them requires learning specific steps to reduce their impact on us. You'll gain valuable skills to become "shrewd as a serpent" and stand with unshakable faith in unsafe situations.

Printed in the USA
CPSIA information can be obtained
at www.ICGtesting.com
JSHW012151051123
51475JS00007B/22

9 781645 085423